# IF LOW TAXES CREATE JOBS,

# WHERE ARE THEY?

# IF LOW TAXES CREATE JOBS, WHERE ARE THEY?

## WHERE ARE THEY?

### The Answer to the Question:
### Do Low Tax Rates Create Jobs?

Robert H. Miller

ISBN:        0-9677480-6-2

ISBN 13    978-0-9677480-6-1

Published By

NOTRAMOUR PRESS

Blairstown, NJ 07825

"Those that fail to learn from history are doomed to repeat it."

—Winston Churchill

# CONTENTS

# 1

# INTRODUCTION

With a title like that you might erroneously conclude that the following treatise will present a predetermined conclusion that low taxes do not create jobs. Not at all. If you take the time to read further, you will find an objective—and most definitely not, ideological—analysis of the question: *Do Low Tax Rates Create More Jobs?* So why the title? My wife suggested a snappier title than the one I was planning to use: Low Tax Rates Create Jobs—Reality or Myth. "Too boring," she said, and she was right. Hopefully the revised title was enough to induce you to look inside. So now that you're here, let's get serious.

Whether you believe low taxes create jobs likely depends upon which side of the ideological divide you stand on. Generally, if you are a conservative Republican, the answer is a resounding yes. On the other hand, if you are a liberal Democrat the answer is an equally resounding no. Or if you're an Independent, as I am, you scratch your head in puzzlement trying to avoid basing a conclusion on which side yells the loudest. And that becomes even more difficult when Party stalwarts present their arguments with such conviction, it becomes easier to believe they are absolute truths.

From the Republicans come a staccato of voices proclaiming that to increase employment levels, not only must we not raise taxes, we must actually lower them. They argue it is high-income earners who create jobs and any attempt to raise the taxes they pay will remove their incentive to invest in new businesses—the source of job creation. The Democrats counter equally vociferously that new investment in business is a function of demand for its product or services, not tax rates, which in a recessionary period can be stimulated by government investments, for example in infrastructure. Then there are numerous other issues—fairness or the progressivity of taxes based on income, benefits to special interests, the role of government and many others—that deepen the quagmire and cause the concerned, but politically independent citizen to throw up his or her hands in frustration. Yet the fundamental question remains. Are more jobs created when income tax rates are low or when they are high? Or to put it somewhat differently, do low income tax rates stimulate job creation.

The answer to this question is not a matter of opinion. And I do not understand why more is not made of the facts that support or refute this premise. After all, there are historical records we can look at to determine whether this correlation actually exists. Now I'm sure there are those who would argue that so many factors must be taken into account that it is virtually impossible to rely simply on the historical record to reach a valid conclusion on this question. There is merit to this contention. Looking at the historical record alone is not likely to provide the answer to *why* the results are what they appear to be. That would undoubtedly prove to be a herculean task for the most experienced and knowledgeable economist and tax professional, let alone a layman—a description to which I humbly acquiesce.

Yet the question remains and deserves an answer. Is there is a way to approach this issue that can produce a reasonable conclusion? I believe so, but before getting too far along, let me tell you a little about who I am and perhaps respond to the most obvious question: What credentials do I have to make such a study and then draw an educated conclusion? Probably not as many as I would like—I am neither a tax professional, economist or statistician—but I believe my background and experience provide a strong foundation from which to analyze information and reach an objective conclusion.

First my politics: I am an independent who has contributed to the campaigns of and voted for both Republicans and Democrats, so I don't have an axe to grind for any political party. My academic credentials: I graduated Cum Laude from Rutgers University more than fifty years ago so I can't say that much I learned then, if indeed I did, provides anything more than a foundation for the experience that followed.

My work experience: I started my career as an accountant working for what was then one of the Big Eight firms, earned my CPA certificate and subsequently moved on to private industry where I eventually wound up as a senior executive. I have enjoyed the trappings of success and the frustration of failure. I know what both feel like and can say unequivocally that success is the much better of the two. I have spent many years in international business and have traveled much of the world. I have interacted personally with factory workers, executives, and celebrities of differing nationalities (even politicians). In short, I have a very broad-based background with a foundation in accounting that enables me to not only understand numbers, but interpret them as well.

In the 1980's I was a Group Vice President and Director of Squibb Corporation before its merger with Bristol-Meyers. My responsibility was for Personal Products where I was the President and CEO of Squibb's Cosmetic and Fragrance Division. In addition to the typical activities of companies engaged in that business, we were very much involved in studying the impact of fragrance on human behavior as well as the ability of fragrance to mask or even dispel odors and cigarette smoke. At that time Dr. Louis Thomas, Chancellor of Memorial Sloan-Kettering Cancer Center and a well-known medical researcher and humanist was also on the Squibb Board of Directors. Before one of our Board meetings he and I had the opportunity to discuss the empirical research in which we were engaged and in which he had previously expressed an interest. He noted that this approach—verifying a conclusion based on observation and experiment rather than on scientific theory—was used in medical research. He added that confirming the relationship of an end result to a given condition was important in and of itself, even without understanding why that relationship existed, and could be of value in ultimately determining the answer to why it existed.

I was reminded of this conversation as I pondered a possible objection to looking solely at the results reflected in the historical records without being able to explain the *"why"* behind them. I realized that Dr. Thomas' observations about empirical research were relevant to the basic issue of whether low tax rates equate to more job creation than otherwise. This view was reinforced when I remembered my early days as an accountant, or more precisely, my first accounting course in college.

After introducing himself with a real or feigned country boy drawl—I never did learn which it was—the professor proceeded to tell this story.

He went to a client's office, looked at the client's financial records and said to him, "I see you had a good year." Then he asked the class, "Anybody here know how I could tell?"

Of course being wide-eyed freshmen and not wanting to sound stupid, no one responded. So he smiled and then gave the answer.

"I looked at his retained earnings at the beginning of the year and his retained earnings at the end of the year. Since his latest retained earnings were much higher, it was clear that the increase was the result of good earnings during the year. I didn't know how he got there, whether it was more sales or lower expenses, but I did know the end result."

For the reader unfamiliar with accounting terminology, here's a quick tutorial. A balance sheet discloses a company's assets, liabilities and net worth (or more technically in a corporation, stockholders' equity). Net worth is the difference between a company's assets and liabilities. Retained earnings are the amount of a company's net worth that relates solely to its earnings from the current and prior years. So back to the professor's principle—if you know the balance sheet is correct at the beginning and end of the year and assuming no changes in stock issuance, the difference in net worth between the two years represents earnings for the year. Obviously an auditor must do more work to assure the accuracy of the financial statements, but this example reinforces the point of looking at conditions at two points in time to determine results for the period in between.

I take time for this introduction to accounting because it exemplifies the methodology used to determine changes in employment. A balance sheet is a snapshot at a point in time. Taking a snapshot at another point in time allows you to determine the changes that have occurred in between—a fact—regardless of what caused it. Thus I have focused on a snapshot of the employment situation at the same point in time in each of the years studied to determine the change that has occurred.

For example, supposing at the end of year one, 140 million individuals were employed and at the end of year two, 143 million were employed. The fact is there were 3 million more people working at the end of year two. Whether they were new jobs, recall from layoffs or any other reason is irrelevant. It is the end result that counts and that is what we will look at when we review tax rates in effect during those periods from different perspectives and different income levels. Then we will attempt to determine whether there is a correlation between tax rates and job creation.

I recognize that there are other factors related to employment that have relevance. For example, the size of the work force compared to the population—the participation rate—indicative of the extent to which individuals have left the labor market—or the number and rate of the unemployed, an equally valid measure in examining the dynamics of the labor market.

I must also emphasize that in discussing tax rates the entire focus is on the highest marginal rates, those relating to taxable incomes of $200,000, $250,000, $400,000 and $1,000,000. No attention is paid to those rates at lower levels (applying to taxable incomes below $200,000). It is a readily apparent conclusion that, as a group, lower income earners generally have more pressing demands on their available funds than investing in new businesses. Even though lower taxes for this group provide more funds available for their buying goods and services, which in itself stimulates the economy and makes them indirect job creators, it is routinely argued that those individuals taxed at the highest rates are the ones who make the investments necessary to create jobs. That is certainly the Republican argument, and though Democrats will not necessarily agree with the latter contention, they will undoubtedly accept the stimulative effect generated by lower taxes on lower wage earners.

Additionally, no consideration has been given to tax rates on investment income, the alternative minimum tax or self-employment taxes, as well as credits for such items as retirement savings contributions.

One might argue, therefore, that because of the factors omitted from this analysis, regardless of the results, the correlation, if any, between tax rates on the highest incomes and job creation are meaningless. I disagree. While these are factors, I do not believe they materially impact the answer to the question asked, and have been intentionally excluded. In essence, I believe that in its simplicity, this focus will enable us to conclude whether there is any correlation between job creation and tax rates.

In a subject such as this that requires examining a multitude of statistics, it is not unusual for eyes to glaze over and the reader to immediately become confused, frustrated, and ultimately disinterested in whatever the writer is trying to demonstrate. So I shall try to summarize the data in a way that presents the conclusions in a manner readily understood, yet with sufficient backup material for anyone with the desire to delve further and test the validity of the data itself and the conclusions reached. Whether I am successful in this endeavor shall rest with you, the reader.

**2**

# GENERAL OUTLINE OF THE STUDY

# EMPLOYMENT

The Bureau of Labor Statistics is an agency within the U.S. Department of Labor whose main role is to provide the government with facts relating to labor economics and statistics. Each month it publishes reports relating to the size of the workforce, the number and rates of the employed and unemployed, and a variety of other statistics on this subject. In addition to covering the United States in its entirety, many reports are also broken down by region, occupation and worker characteristics including age, sex, race and others.

There are two principal sources for these reports: The Current Population Survey (CPS), also known as the household survey, and the Current Employment Statistics (CES) survey, also known as the establishment or payroll survey. The U.S. Census Bureau conducts both surveys.

The CPS, which measures the extent of employment and unemployment in the country, has been conducted every month since 1940 and has been expanded and modified several times since then. In July 2011 the sample was increased from 50,000 to 60,000 eligible households, covering approximately 110,000 individuals.

The CES provides monthly estimates of employment, hours, and earnings on a national, state and major metropolitan area basis derived from a survey covering approximately 141,000 businesses and government agencies and approximately 486,000 workers.

Both surveys are conducted as of the 12th day of the month. The CPS criteria is the labor status of household members in the sample during the week in which the 12th day of the month occurs, whereas the CES criteria is the number of persons on payrolls in the sample who received pay during the pay period that includes the 12th day of the month.

Both surveys use different definitions of employment with the CPS providing a more expansive classification including, for example, self-employed persons, private household workers, and workers in the agricultural sector, all of which are excluded from the CES.

For the purpose of this study I have used the more expansive data from the CPS to examine any correlation with tax rates, and have chosen the January report of each year as the snapshot in time to measure changes in employment. Since the 12th of the following January is closer to the previous December 31st than is the 12th of that December, this report provides a somewhat better measure of a year's results. Also, since it is fair to say that tax rates are closely related to the philosophy and policies of the president then in office, it is also useful to look at employment results for the comparable period.

As a presidential term begins on January 20th, the January report provides a basis to also correlate data to each presidential term of office. For example, January 1953 is the base, or first year for Eisenhower's term in office and January 1961 is his last and Kennedy's base year. One could reasonably argue that the base year should be the January succeeding a president's inauguration since it is not realistic to presume a president can influence the labor market to any great extent during his first year, even though a President can influence tax rates in that first year. While both arguments are reasonable. I will relate data to the president from the year of his inauguration to the conclusion of his term. Other than to provide ammunition to those who wish to prove their favorite Republican or Democratic president produced the most jobs, I do not believe this will fundamentally affect the conclusions reached as to whether low taxes create more jobs than otherwise.

# 3

# TAX RATES

There are three different categories of taxes that need to be examined to determine whether there is any correlation to employment changes. They are the individual income tax, capital gains—even though it is an inherent element of the individual income tax—and the corporate income tax.

An individual's federal income tax is based on his or her taxable income, which is determined after inclusion or exclusion of certain types of income and then allowing for certain deductions and exemptions from that income. There are different tax schedules that apply to different classifications of people. While those classifications have changed somewhat since 1953, today they are: Single; Married filing jointly or Qualifying widow(s); Married filing separately; and Head of Household. Within each classification there are brackets (or ranges) of taxable income with a base amount of tax that relates to the lower of the two taxable incomes and then a rate that is applied to the amount by which actual taxable income exceeds the lower of the two taxable incomes in that bracket. There is a maximum rate applied to each bracket of taxable income and a maximum rate applied to income that exceeds the highest income tax bracket.

For the purpose of this study I have used tax rates for the "Married filing jointly" classification or the classification in earlier years that included married couples filing jointly. Use of the term individual or individuals in the context of tax rates refers to a married couple and not a single individual.

The term, Maximum Income Tax Rate or maximum rate, used frequently herein, refers to the highest annual tax rate applied to a married couple's specific taxable income level ($1,000,000, $400,000, $250,000 or $200,000).

Since income tax rates are directly related to an individual's taxable income, maximum rates can vary based on the structure of the tax brackets. For example, the highest rates on the 2008 IRS Tax Table for a married couple filing jointly are shown in Exhibit 1. In this example the highest maximum rate is 35% and is applied to taxable income in excess of $357,700, which, therefore, would include taxable incomes of $1,000,000 and $400,000. However, the maximum rate for individuals whose taxable income was $250,000 (more than $200,300 but less than $357,700) was 33%, while for those whose taxable income was $200,000 (more than $131,450 but less than $200,300), the maximum rate was 28%.

On the other hand, in 1984 the highest taxable income bracket—equivalent to the $357,700 in 2008—was $162,400, so that the maximum rate for all levels of taxable income that exceeded this amount was 50%.

Exhibit 1

**Extract from 2008 Tax Rate Tables**

| If your taxable income is | | The Tax is | of the amount |
|---|---|---|---|
| Over | But not over | | over |
| 131,450 | 200,300 | $25,550 + 28% | 131,450 |
| 200,300 | 357,700 | 44,828 + 33% | 200,300 |
| 357,700 | | 96,770 + 35% | 257,700 |

**Source: 2008 IRS Tax Rate Tables**

Individual income tax rates used herein are derived from Internal Revenue Service Instructions to Form 1040 and Tax Rate Tables of the respective years for married individuals, filing jointly. Sources for capital gains and corporate income tax rates are listed on the respective Appendices.

# 4

# ACCUMULATION AND PRESENTATION OF DATA

It is beyond question that the U.S. tax code is extremely complex. It is even more so when one tries to compare individual income tax rates in effect over a period of 59 years given the differing income levels at which those rates take effect. Nevertheless, we will look at the maximum rates in effect each year as well as changes in maximum rates from one year to the next. To calculate an increase or decrease can be as simple as looking at the maximum tax rates each year and seeing whether they went up or down from the preceding year, although an actual tax decrease or increase can occur when income brackets change despite no change in the maximum rates.

The results thus obtained have been related to employment data derived from BLS reports based on the January CPS (household survey) in the respective years and then grouped into meaningful categories to ascertain whether a correlation exists.

Later we will also look at the Effective Income Tax Rate, or effective rate, in a similar manner to take account of the effect of bracket changes year to year, surcharges and inflation adjustments and relate them to employment data for each year.

We will also relate annual capital gains tax rates and maximum corporate income tax rates to their respective annual employment data.

Exhibits summarizing the data are shown within the text and are each supported by supplemental Appendices that show the source of the original data and then how it has been summarized for the related Exhibit. The reader can stop at the summary Exhibits or go as far back as he or she desires to see the original data, or even back to the source of the data itself, which is disclosed in the respective Appendices.

The question—do low tax rates produce more jobs than otherwise—will be addressed by comparing employment increases or decreases to differing classifications of tax rates in effect in their respective years and then grouping the results to determine whether a pattern exists and a reasonable conclusion can be drawn.

Employment data has been recorded from January 1953 to January 2012, and tax data from 1953 to 2011, or a total of 59 years in each case. I would suggest that this is a long enough period from which to draw conclusions if, indeed, there are conclusions to be drawn.

# 5

# HISTORICAL MAXIMUM TAX RATES
# AND EMPLOYMENT INCREASES AND DECREASES

In Exhibit 2 employment increases and decreases are summarized according to a range of Maximum Individual Income Tax Rates, or the highest marginal rates then in effect in their respective years. Appendix A 1.1 incudes details of the data by year and Appendix A 1.2 then shows the same data sorted by the top marginal tax rate. It is this latter schedule from which the groups, or range of tax rates, are developed.

Exhibit 2

| Maximum Tax Rates 1953-2011 | | | | | |
|---|---|---|---|---|---|
| Comparison to Best, Worst and Average Employment Increases (Decreases) | | | | | |
| Range of Maximum Tax Rates* | Number Years | Average Maximum Tax Rates | Employment Increase (Decrease) (In thousands) | | |
| | | | Best | Worst | Average |
| 28% - 31% | 5 | 29.2% | 2,692 | (1,141) | 1,012 |
| 35.0% | 9 | 35% | 2,905 | (4,210) | 469 |
| 38.5% -39.6% | 11 | 39% | 3,532 | (2,077) | 1,946 |
| 50.0% | 5 | 50% | 4,040 | (531) | 2,252 |
| 70% - 77.0% | 18 | 70% | 4,456 | (928) | 1,743 |
| 91% - 92% | 11 | 91.1% | 3,000 | (1,576) | 612 |
| * Excludes surcharges and credit from rates where applicable | | | | | |
| See Appendix A 1.2 | | | | | |

Maximum rates of 28% to 31% were in effect over a five-year period in which the average rate was 29.2%. During those five years the worst performance, or the largest number of jobs lost, came when employment fell by 1,141,000 jobs. The best performance, or the greatest number of jobs created, saw employment rise by 2,692,000 jobs, while the average number of jobs created when maximum rates were between 28% and 31% was 1,012,000.

*It is interesting to note that the greatest decrease in employment in the last 59 years occurred in 2008—4,210,000 jobs—when the maximum rate was 35%, while the greatest increase in employment occurred in 1977—4,456,000 jobs—when the maximum individual tax rate was 70%.* One could argue that the 2008 decrease transpired as the worst recession since the Great Depression was emerging and should be disregarded, particularly since there were five years of employment growth preceding it. The counter argument is that the 2008 decrease was followed in 2009 by a further decrease of 3,687,000 jobs, which substantially reduced the employment gains of those previous years and during which the maximum tax rate was also 35%.

On the other hand, 1977, the year in which the best increase in employment over 59 years was recorded was preceded by two years and followed by three years of employment growth. When the employment numbers did turn negative in 1981, 263,000 jobs were lost, followed by an additional loss of 531,000 jobs in 1982 before turning positive again in 1983. During the years of positive growth (1975 to 1980) the maximum rate was 70%, as it was in 1981 (the year of an employment decrease). In 1982, despite a decrease in the tax rate to 50%, the number of jobs declined.

The point of this discussion is to emphasize that each year's employment results must stand on its own. One can always rationalize away results that don't support his or her point of view. But over a 59-year period the results speak for themselves.

The largest average increase in jobs—2,252.000—occurred when maximum tax rates were at 50% followed by average increases in jobs of 1,946,000 and 1,743,000 when maximum tax rates ranged from a low of 38.5% to a high of 77%. When tax rates exceeded 91%, the average employment increase was 612,000 jobs, still better than the average increase of 469,000 when the maximum rate was 35%, though not as good as the 1,012,000 increase when the maximum rate averaged 29.2%.

Exhibit 3 presents this same information differently, showing the total amount of jobs created and the total lost as well as the overall net increase in employment for each of the same range of maximum rates as in Exhibit 2. The reclassified numbers indicate a somewhat similar pattern of a greater number of jobs created at the higher end of maximum rates. For example, in the same number of years (5) when maximum rates averaged 50%, the number of jobs created were more than double those created when maximum rates were 29.2%—11,261,000 compared to 5,059,000. And despite a maximum rate range that averaged 70.4% over 18 years, or more than twice that of the maximum rate range that averaged 35% over 9 years, employment increased by more than 7 times—31,365,000 jobs compared to 4,220,000. This latter result was fueled by more than 6 times the number of jobs lost when maximum rate were at 35%, and by twice the number of jobs created when maximum rates were at 70.4%

Exhibit 3

| Average Maximum Tax Rates 1953-2011 | | | | | |
|---|---|---|---|---|---|
| Comparison to Total and Net Employment Increases (Decreases) | | | | | |
| Range of Maximum Tax Rates* | Number Years | Average Maximum Tax Rates | Employment Net Increase (Decrease) (thousands) | Employment Total | |
| | | | | Increase (thousands) | Decrease (thousands) |
| 28% - 31% | 5 | 29.2% | 5,059 | 6,200 | (1,141) |
| 35.0% | 9 | 35.0% | 4,220 | 12,117 | (7,897) |
| 38.5% -39.6% | 11 | 39.4% | 21,405 | 23,482 | (2,077) |
| 50.0% | 5 | 50.0% | 11,261 | 11,792 | (531) |
| 70% - 77.0% | 18 | 70.4% | 31,365 | 32,556 | (1,191) |
| 91% - 92% | 11 | 91.1% | 6,727 | 8,836 | (2,109) |
| * Excludes surcharges and credit from rates where applicable | | | | | |
| See Appendices A 2.3 and A 2.4 | | | | | |

Since today's proponents of lower taxes argue that current rates are too high and need to be lowered, it seems appropriate to classify the maximum rates at or below the current rate of 35% as "lower rates" and all rates above that as higher. Using this classification, *the historical record indicates clearly that more jobs were created when higher marginal rates were in effect.*

Is this the final answer? Not really. We have been looking at employment changes compared to static tax rates in effect for the relevant period; however the reasonable question that follows is whether there is a different conclusion if we look at employment results when tax rates were lowered or raised.

# 6

# CHANGES IN HISTORICAL MAXIMUM TAX RATES
# AND EMPLOYMENT INCREASES AND DECREASES

In Exhibit 4 we look at employment increases and decreases that occurred in the year in which the highest maximum individual tax rates were changed and the subsequent two years to measure whether the change had more lasting effect than just in that one year. Here the results generally show a more favorable picture for the positive effect a lowering of maximum rates have on employment.

Exhibit 4

| Reductions in Maximum Tax Rates 1953-2011 | | | | | |
|---|---|---|---|---|---|
| Comparison to Employment Increases (Decreases) | | | | | |
| In Year of Change and Subsequent Two Years | | | | | |
| Year of Change | Change in Maximum Tax Rate | Employment Increase (Decrease) (thousands) | Employment Increase (Decrease) | | |
| | | | Year of Change | I Year Later | 2 Years Later |
| 1982 | -20.0% | (531) | (531) | 4,040 | 3,101 |
| 1964 | -14.0% | 1,670 | 1,670 | 2,201 | 1,473 |
| 1987 | -11.5% | 3,063 | 3,063 | 2,692 | 2,373 |
| 1988* | -10.5% | 2,692 | 2,692 | 2,373 | (1,141) |
| 1965 | -7.0% | 2,201 | 2,201 | 1,473 | 1,029 |
| 2003 | -3.6% | 1,055 | 1,055 | 1,773 | 2,905 |
| 1954 | -1.0% | 729 | 729 | 3,000 | (121) |
| 2001 | -0.5% | (2,077) | (2,077) | 1,716 | 1,055 |
| 2002 | -0.5% | 1,716 | 1,716 | 1,055 | 1,773 |
| 9 | -68.6% | 10,518 | Total | | |
| | -7.6% | 1,169 | Average | | |
| See Appendix A 3.3 | | | | | |
| * Rate changes exclude imposition and/or removal of surcharge | | | | | |

In 1982 the top marginal individual tax rate was lowered by 20%

(actually 20 percentage points), the largest single decrease in taxes in the 59-year period under study. Initially the results were disappointing with a loss of 531,000 jobs the first year. However, this was followed by an increase in jobs of 4,040,000 and 3,101,000 in the next two years, respectively. Comparable results were achieved in other years with most showing employment increases in the year of change as well as in the subsequent two years.

Excluding the removal of tax surcharges, there were 9 years between 1953 and 2011 when the maximum rate was lowered directly, accounting for an increase of 10,518,000 jobs in the year of change, or an average of 1,169,000 jobs per year based on an average decrease of 7.6% in the tax rate. Though there were a few instances of a loss of jobs in the year of rate change and the second subsequent year, it is fair to say that lowering the top marginal individual tax rate had a beneficial effect on employment. That seems to change the conclusion reached earlier. Perhaps it is the lowering of the maximum rate that is the answer to creating jobs. But is it?

We've seen what happened when tax rates were lowered; so the obvious next question is how did employment react when the maximum rate was raised? Surprisingly, no differently, as shown in Exhibit 5.

Exhibit 5

| Increases in Maximum Tax Rates 1953-2011 Comparison to Employment Increase (Decrease) In Year of Change and Subsequent Two Years | | | | | |
|---|---|---|---|---|---|
| Year of Change | Change in Maximum Tax Rate | Employment Increase (Decrease) (thousands) | Employment Increase (Decrease) | | |
| | | | Year of Change | I Year Later | 2 Years Later |
| 1991 | 3.0% | 38 | 38 | 1,097 | 2,891 |
| 1993 | 8.6% | 2,891 | 2,891 | 2,697 | 462 |
| 2 | 11.6% | 2,929 | Total | | |
| | 5.8% | 1,465 | Average | | |
| See Appendix A 3.3 * Rate changes exclude imposition and removal of surcharge | | | | | |

Again, excluding the imposition of a surcharge, maximum rates were raised twice in the 59-year period. The largest single increase—8.6%—occurred in 1993 and produced 2,891,000 jobs in the year of change and 2,697,000 and 462,000 jobs, respectively in the subsequent two years. For the 2 years, the rate increase averaged 5.8% and created an average of 1,465,000 jobs. Significantly, there were no decreases in employment in the year of change or subsequent two years for any of the 2 tax increases.

Exhibit 6

| Largest Maximum Tax Rate Decreases and Increases 1953-2011 Comparison to Employment Increases (Decreases) In Year of Change and Subsequent Two Years | | | | | |
|---|---|---|---|---|---|
| Year of Change | Change in Maximum Tax Rate | Employment Increase (Decrease) (thousands) | Employment Increase (Decrease) | | |
| | | | Year of Change | 1 Year Later | 2 Years Later |
| Reduction in Maximum Tax Rates | | | | | |
| 1982 | -20.0% | (531) | (531) | 4,040 | 3,101 |
| 1964 | -14.0% | 1,670 | 1,670 | 2,201 | 1,473 |
| 1987 | -11.5% | 3,063 | 3,063 | 2,692 | 2,373 |
| 1988* | -10.5% | 2,692 | 2,692 | 2,373 | (1,141) |
| 4 | -14.0% | 1,724 | 1,724 | 2,827 | 1,452 |
| Increase in Maximum Tax Rates | | | | | |
| 1993 | 8.60% | 2,891 | 2,891 | 2,697 | 462 |
| See Exhibits 4 and 5 | | | | | |

Comparing results of rate reductions to rate increases, we find that, on average, more jobs were created when rates were increased (1,465,000 jobs) than when rates were decreased (1,169,000 jobs). Exhibit 6 demonstrates that taking only the top 4 rate reductions—those in excess of 10%—brings the average rate decrease up to 14% and the average increase in jobs up to 1,724,000. On the surface this would suggest that it is the larger rate reductions that create more jobs. True, but one could just as accurately argue that if only the single largest tax increase of 8.6% was considered, on average, the 4 largest tax rate decreases did not produce more jobs than the single largest tax increase. This is not the result anticipated and is counter intuitive to what one might reasonably expect.

Since there have been surcharges imposed and removed several times in this 59-year period and one credit applied, these need to be examined to see whether they materially impact the results observed thus far. However, because these additional charges and credits were applied to a calculated tax amount, they did not change the rates themselves. Accordingly, we will look at them shortly in the context of changes in the effective tax rate (for taxable incomes of $1,000,000 and $250,000).

Before doing so, there is another avenue to explore. Thus far we have looked at decreases in rates over 9 years and increases over 2 years, leaving 48 years with no changes in the maximum rates from one year to the next. To see how employment reacted when maximum rates were not changed, we look at Exhibit 7.

Exhibit 7

| No Change in Maximum Tax Rates 1953-2011 Comparison to Employment Increases (Decreases) | | | |
|---|---|---|---|
| Years | Range of Employment Increases (Decreases) (thousands) | Total Employment Increases (Decreases) (thousands) | Average Employment Increases (Decreases) (thousands) |
| Employment increases | | | |
| 2 | 4,000 - 4,999 | 8,496 | 4,248 |
| 6 | 3,000 - 3,999 | 19,764 | 3,294 |
| 13 | 2.000 - 2,999 | 31,470 | 2,421 |
| 10 | 1,000 - 1,999 | 15,004 | 1,500 |
| 9 | 1 - 999 | 4,194 | 466 |
| 40 | All | 78,928 | 1,973 |
| Employment Decreases | | | |
| 8 | All | (12,338) | (1,542) |
| Net Employment Change | | | |
| 48 | All | 66,590 | 1,387 |
| See Appendix A 3.4 | | | |

In 40 of those years employment increased by 78,928,000 jobs and in 8 years decreased by 12,338,000 jobs, or a net increase of 66,590,000 jobs.

On average, that comes to an increase of 1,387,000 jobs annually over the 48 years, which is greater than the 9-year average annual increase of 1,169,000 jobs when rates were reduced. *So while we have produced evidence that demonstrates that decreases in the highest maximum rates do produce employment gains, we have also seen that better results have been achieved in the few instances when there were increases in maximum rates and indeed, even when there were no changes at all in the maximum rate.*

# 7

# HISTORICAL EFFECTIVE TAX RATES
# AND EMPLOYMENT INCREASES AND DECREASES

As indicated earlier, looking at maximum rates alone is only part of the story when looking at the impact rates have on employment. Given the graduated or progressive nature of the tax structure, tax decreases can be achieved without changing rates by simply widening tax brackets. For example in 1978 and 1979 the maximum rate was 70%—no change in rates from one year to the next. Yet there was an acknowledged tax decrease as explained in the "Highlights for 1979" section included in the IRS booklet, *1979 Instructions for preparing Form 1040.*

> **"Tax Rates Have Been Decreased
> and Personal Exemptions Have
> Been Increased**
>
> For most taxpayers, the tax rates have
> been decreased. The deduction for
> personal exemptions has been increased
> from $750 to $1,000. This increase
> also applies to the extra exemptions for
> age and blindness. . . ."

Thus, to provide a more expansive view of the impact on employment, we will now examine the **effective** income tax rate for the same married couple filing jointly. Note that this rate relates solely to taxable income and, therefore, will always be higher than the effective rate based on total or adjusted gross income.

The effective rate is determined by dividing the calculated amount of tax by the related taxable income. This calculation takes into account the impact of tax surcharges or credits, which are not reflected in the maximum rates since the maximum rate is applied to the taxable income that exceeds a base amount whereas tax surcharges can apply to the entire amount of tax.

For example, in 1970 when the maximum rate was 70%, a surcharge of 10% of the calculated tax was assessed. In that year the base tax for $250,000 taxable income was $110,980 and the excess over $200,000 ($50,000) was taxed at 70%, or $35,000, bringing the total tax before the surcharge to $145,980. Applying the 10% surcharge to that amount increases the total tax to $160,578. But if the surcharge were applied to the maximum rate of 70%, bringing that rate to 77%, and applied to the $50,000 excess, the excess tax would rise to $38,500, but the total tax would fall to $149,480 resulting in an underpayment of $11,098, despite the obvious preference for the latter calculation by those subject to the surcharge.

Looking at the effective rate also allows the effect of inflation adjustments to be considered against changes in employment.

Exhibit 8

| Average Maximum and Effective Income Tax Rates 1953-2011 Comparison to Employment Increases (Decreases) By Maximum Income Tax Rate | | | | | | |
|---|---|---|---|---|---|---|
| Years | Average Employment Increase (Decrease) (thousands) | Average Maximum Income Tax Rate | Average Effective Income Tax Rates on Taxable Incomes of | | | |
| | | | $1,000,000 | $400,000 | $250,000 | $200,000 |
| 5 | 1,012 | 29.2% | 29.0% | 28.7% | 28.4% | 28.1% |
| 9 | 469 | 35.0% | 32.2% | 28.1% | 24.7% | 22.8% |
| 11 | 1,946 | 39.4% | 36.9% | 33.2% | 29.9% | 28.3% |
| 5 | 2,252 | 50.0% | 48.3% | 45.7% | 43.1% | 41.3% |
| 18 | 1,743 | 70.4% | 68.0% | 63.4% | 58.9% | 55.8% |
| 11 | 612 | 91.1% | 86.5% | 79.7% | 73.5% | 69.5% |
| See Appendices A 4.3 and A 4.4 | | | | | | |

We have already looked at the highest maximum rate in effect during each year compared to employment changes in that year. Now we will look at the actual effective rate in each year based on taxable incomes of $1,000,000, $400,000, $250,000 and $200,000, which have been referred to as incomes of the job creators.

Effective tax rates for each year have been calculated for the above taxable incomes along with the related employment increase or decrease for that year and are shown in summary in Exhibit 8. While employment changes are shown, the analysis of average maximum rates follows that of Exhibit 3 and would elicit similar comments. The purpose of this Exhibit is to demonstrate the general relationship between the maximum rates over these last 59 years and the effective rates at differing job creator income levels.

Exhibit 9

| Average Effective Tax Rates 1953-2011 | | | | | |
|---|---|---|---|---|---|
| Based on Taxable Income of $1,000,000 | | | | | |
| Comparison to Average and Total Employment Increases (Decreases) | | | | | |
| Average Maximum Individual Tax Rate | Average* Effective Individual Tax Rate | Number Years | Average Employment Increase (thousands) | Employment Total | |
| | | | | Increase (thousands) | Decrease (thousands) |
| 29.2% | 29.0% | 5 | 1,012 | 6,200 | (1,141) |
| 35.0% | 32.2% | 9 | 469 | 12,117 | (7,897) |
| 39.4% | 36.9% | 11 | 1,946 | 23,482 | (2,077) |
| 50.0% | 48.3% | 5 | 2,252 | 11,792 | (531) |
| 70.4% | 68.0% | 18 | 1,743 | 32,556 | (1,191) |
| 91.1% | 86.5% | 11 | 612 | 8,836 | (2,109) |
| *Includes surcharges and credit in effective tax rates where applicable | | | | | |
| See Appendices A 5.3 and A 5.4 | | | | | |

Detailed analysis has been done for taxable incomes of $1,000,000 and $250,000 to demonstrate employment results related to income, the former having always been subject to the maximum tax rate and the latter, the level presented by many as the base for job creation. Note also that, as said earlier, the effective rates reflect surcharges and one credit that are not reflected in the maximum rates. Notwithstanding the many differences year to year in deductions, exclusions, inclusions and exemptions, effective tax rates are a more accurate reflection of what individuals actually pay in tax, mindful that this rate is based on taxable rather than total or adjusted gross income. As such, it offers another basis of comparison of rates to employment.

Exhibit 9 compares employment increases and decreases with related effective rates based on taxable income of $1,000,000. As might be expected with a taxable income level that has always been subject to maximum rates, total employment increases and decreases and average employment increases mirror those of the highest maximum rates in Exhibits 2 and 3, bringing us to the same conclusions: *employment increased significantly more, both in total and on average, at higher effective rates than at lower rates.* In fact, if you combine the results for the two lowest sets of average tax brackets—29% and 32.2%—the net employment increase over those 14 years was 9,279,000 jobs, which equates to an annual average of 663,000 jobs.

Exhibit 10

| Lowest and Highest Average Effective Tax Rates 1953-2011 | | | | | |
|---|---|---|---|---|---|
| Based on Taxable Income of $1,000,000 | | | | | |
| Comparison to Average and Total Employment Increases (Decreases) | | | | | |
| Average Maximum Individual Tax Rate | Average* Effective Individual Tax Rate | Number Years | Net Employment Increase (thousands) | Employment Total Increase (thousands) | Decrease (thousands) |
| Lowest average effective rates | | | | | |
| 29.2% | 29.0% | 5 | 5,059 | 6,200 | (1,141) |
| 35.0% | 32.2% | 9 | 4,220 | 12,117 | (7,897) |
| | Total | 14 | 9,279 | 18,317 | (9,038) |
| | Average | | 663 | 1,308 | (646) |
| Highest average effective rates | | | | | |
| 91.1% | 86.5% | 11 | 612 | 8,836 | (2,109) |
| ** Includes surcharges and credit in effective tax rates where applicable | | | | | |
| See Appendices A 5.3 and A 5.4 | | | | | |

The only period when worse results occurred—612,000 jobs annually—was when the average maximum rate was 91.1% and effective rate 86.5%. So with rates of 29.2% and 35.0% that were, at least, 56% percentage points lower than the maximum rates, only 51,000, or 8.3%, more jobs were generated annually.

One final point before moving on. Note the closeness of the effective rates to the highest maximum rates at the taxable income level of $1,000,000. This is important as the structure of tax brackets generally results in greater differences between the highest maximum rate and effective rate as taxable income decreases. Which, of course, makes sense since graduated rates—the greater your income, the greater the rate at which you pay tax—is the basis of our tax system. This will become quite clear as we next look at the effective rates for taxable income of $250,000.

This income level is in the news today as it represents a break point at which some believe current tax rates should be increased, at least to the levels that existed during the Clinton presidency, prior to the reductions made in the subsequent Bush presidency. Some believe the breakpoint should be $1,000,000, while others argue that no tax rates should be raised from their current levels. We will examine this issue later.

Exhibit 11

| Average Effective Tax Rates 1953-2011 | | | | | |
|---|---|---|---|---|---|
| Based on Taxable Income of $250,000 | | | | | |
| Comparison to Average and Total Employment Increases (Decreases) | | | | | |
| Average Maximum Tax Rates | Average* Effective Tax Rates | Number Years | Average Employment Increase (thousands) | Employment Total Increase (thousands) | Decrease (thousands) |
| 35.0% | 24.7% | 9 | 469 | 12,117 | (7,897) |
| 32.0% | 28.3% | 7 | 671 | 7,916 | (3,218) |
| 39.5% | 30.2% | 9 | 2,418 | 21,766 | 0 |
| 50.0% | 43.1% | 5 | 2,252 | 11,792 | (531) |
| 70.4% | 58.9% | 18 | 1,743 | 32,556 | (1,191) |
| 91.1% | 73.5% | 11 | 612 | 8,836 | (2,109) |
| * Includes surcharges and credit in effective tax rates where applicable | | | | | |
| See Appendix A 7.3 and Appendix A 7.4 | | | | | |

As we look at Exhibit 11, we begin to see some differences with our earlier charts. First is the obvious difference between the average highest maximum rate and effective rate ranging from a low differential of 3.7% and a high of 17.6%. Why is this significant? It demonstrates that it is not just the highest maximum rate that must be examined, but also the structure of the related tax brackets. This will become quite clear when we shortly look at the effective rate within the current highest maximum rate of 35%.

In Exhibit 9 listing average effective tax rates for $1,000,000 in taxable income, the lowest effective rate (29.0%) corresponded directly with the lowest maximum rate (29.2%). Not so for the effective rates for $250,000 taxable income. Here the lowest average maximum rate of 32% produces an average effective rate of 28.3% while the higher maximum rate of 35% equates to an average effective rate of 24.7%. This means that the current highest maximum rate of 35% offers a lower effective rate at the taxable income level of $250,000 than the lower 32% maximum rate. This will be discussed in a different context later, but it also has significance when comparing tax rates to employment increases and decreases.

Despite the lowest effective rates at the $250,000 income level in the 59 years of this study (and many years before), the net average annual increase of 469,000 jobs was the lowest. Note that the sequence of this chart was based on the effective rates, not maximum rates, from the lowest to the highest, which, as explained earlier, is why it differs with preceding charts. *Again, we find that more jobs have been created when the average effective rate exceeded 30.3% and the average maximum rate 39.5%.*

But let's continue and see if reductions in the effective rate when maximum rates are reduced change the narrative in any way. Before doing so, a word of caution. As indicated earlier, reductions in effective rates with no corresponding reduction in maximum rates are usually due to adjustments for inflation. But as explained previously, such changes, even rather small ones, can also be the result of a conscious effort to reduce the tax burden unrelated to inflation. Why such a distinction?

In looking at this issue I believe it is important to distinguish between those changes that are designed to reduce the tax burden so that one actually pays a lesser amount of tax irrespective of inflation and those changes that allow an individual to avoid paying a higher (progressive) tax because inflation has pushed that income to a higher bracket. In essence the latter changes are "inflation deflators" and should not be considered tax reductions.

Exhibit 12

| | | | Change in | Employment | Decrease in | Increase in |
|---|---|---|---|---|---|---|
| | Maximum | Effective* Tax Rate | Effective | Increase (Decrease) | Effective | Effective |
| Year | Tax Rate | $1,000,000 | Tax Rate | (thousands) | Tax Rate | Tax Rate |
| 1982 | 50.0% | 48.7% | -17.1% | (531) | (531) | |
| 1964 | 77.0% | 73.4% | -12.6% | 1,670 | 1,670 | |
| 1987 | 38.5% | 37.5% | -10.5% | 3,063 | 3,063 | |
| 1988* | 28.0% | 28.1% | -9.4% | 2,692 | 2,692 | |
| 1965 | 70.0% | 67.1% | -6.3% | 2,201 | 2,201 | |
| 1970* | 70.0% | 68.8% | -5.0% | 84 | 84 | |
| 2003 | 35.0% | 32.5% | -3.2% | 1,055 | 1,055 | |
| 1955 | 91.0% | 86.0% | -2.5% | 3,000 | 3,000 | |
| 1971 | 70.0% | 67.1% | -1.7% | 2,095 | 2,095 | |
| 1954 | 91.0% | 88.5% | -1.2% | 729 | 729 | |
| 1981* | 70.0% | 65.8% | -0.8% | (263) | (263) | |
| 2002 | 38.6% | 35.7% | -0.6% | 1,716 | 1,716 | |
| 2001 | 39.1% | 36.3% | -0.6% | (2,077) | (2,077) | |
| 1977 | 70.0% | 66.9% | -0.2% | 4,456 | 4,456 | |
| 1979 | 70.0% | 66.7% | -0.2% | 1,931 | 1,931 | |
| 1969* | 70.0% | 73.8% | 1.7% | 1,975 | | 1,975 |
| 1991 | 31.0% | 30.3% | 2.2% | 38 | | 38 |
| 1968* | 70.0% | 72.1% | 5.0% | 2,105 | | 2,105 |
| 1993 | 39.6% | 37.3% | 7.0% | 2,891 | | 2,891 |
| | | | Total | 28,830 | 21,821 | 7,009 |
| | | | Average | 1,517 | 1,455 | 1,752 |

Change in Effective Tax Rates - $1,0000,000 Taxable Income 1953-2011
Result of Decreases and Increases in Effective Tax Rate
Comparison to Employment Increases (Decreases)

* Includes surcharges and credit in effective tax rates where applicable
See Appendix A 6.5

Exhibit 13

| | | | Change in | Employment | Decrease | Increase |
| | | Effective* | in | Increase | in | in |
| | Maximum | Tax Rate | Effective | (Decrease) | Effective | Effective |
| Year | Tax Rate | $250,000 | Tax Rate | (thousands) | Tax Rate | Tax Rate |
|---|---|---|---|---|---|---|
| 1982 | 50.0% | 45.0% | -11.0% | (531) | (531) | |
| 1955 | 91.0% | 71.7% | -9.3% | 3,000 | 3,000 | |
| 1964 | 77.0% | 62.8% | -8.9% | 1,670 | 1,670 | |
| 1987 | 38.5% | 34.5% | -7.5% | 3,063 | 3,063 | |
| 1988* | 28.0% | 28.5% | -6.0% | 2,692 | 2,692 | |
| 1965 | 70.0% | 58.4% | -4.4% | 2,201 | 2,201 | |
| 1970* | 70.0% | 59.9% | -4.4% | 84 | 84 | |
| 2003 | 35.0% | 25.6% | -2.1% | 1,055 | 1,055 | |
| 1954 | 91.0% | 80.9% | -1.8% | 729 | 729 | |
| 1971 | 70.0% | 58.4% | -1.5% | 2,095 | 2,095 | |
| 1979 | 70.0% | 56.7% | -1.1% | 1,931 | 1,931 | |
| 2002 | 38.6% | 27.7% | -0.9% | 1,716 | 1,716 | |
| 1981 | 70.0% | 56.0% | -0.7% | (263) | (263) | |
| 1977 | 70.0% | 57.7% | -0.6% | 4,456 | 4,456 | |
| 2001 | 39.1% | 28.6% | -0.6% | (2,077) | (2,077) | |
| 1991 | 31.0% | 28.2% | -0.2% | 38 | 38 | |
| 1969* | 70.0% | 64.2% | 1.5% | 1,975 | | 1,975 |
| 1993 | 39.6% | 30.2% | 2.5% | 2,891 | | 2,891 |
| 1968* | 196800.0% | 62.8% | 4.4% | 2,105 | | 2,105 |
| | | | Total | 28,830 | 21,859 | 6,971 |
| | | | Average | 1,517 | 1,366 | 2,324 |

Change in Effective Tax Rates - $250,000 Taxable Income 1953-2011
Result of Decreases and Increases in Effective Tax Rate
Comparison to Employment Increases (Decreases)

* Includes surcharges and credit in effective tax rates where applicable

See Appendix A 8.5

In any event we will look at changes in effective rates in three ways and compare them to employment increases and decreases: Actual tax increases and decreases, reductions resulting from inflation adjustments and no changes in the effective rates.

Exhibit 12 summarizes the changes in effective rates and employment that occurred when tax rates were reduced for taxable incomes of $1,000,000, and Exhibit 13 displays the same information for taxable incomes of $250,000. In 1982 the highest maximum rate for both $1,000,000 and $250,000 was reduced from 70% to 50%, a decrease of 20 percentage points. However, the effective rate for $1,000,000 taxable income dropped from 65.8% to 48.7%, a decrease of 17.1 percentage points, while the effective rate for $250,000 taxable income dropped from 56% to 45%, a decrease of 11 percentage points.

The opposite is true in 1955 when despite the maximum rate remaining flat at 91%, the widening of the top bracket from $200,000 to $400,000 brought the effective rate for $250,000 down 9.3 percentage points, while only 2.5 percentage points for $1,000,000.

Exhibit 14

| Change in Effective Income Tax Rates - $1,000,000 Taxable Income | | | | | | |
|---|---|---|---|---|---|---|
| Result of Inflation Adjustments 1953-2011 | | | | | | |
| Comparison to Employment Increases (Decreases) | | | | | | |
| Years | Maximum Income Tax Rate | Effective Tax Rate $1,000,000 Taxable Income | Change in Effective Tax Rate | Employment (thousands) | | |
| | | | | Increase (Decrease) | Increase | Decrease |
| 11 | 33.4% | 31.3% | -0.1% | 5,494 | 14,532 | (9,038) |
| 7 | 39.6% | 37.0% | -0.1% | 15,812 | 15,812 | 0 |
| 4 | 50.0% | 48.1% | -0.2% | 11,792 | 11,792 | 0 |
| | | | Total | 33,098 | 42,136 | (9,038) |
| | | | Average | 1,504 | 2,218 | (3,013) |
| See Appendix A 6.6 | | | | | | |

As stated earlier, since the effective rate is determined by dividing the tax by the taxable income, we can also take account of surcharges assessed or a credit granted against the calculated tax, which cannot be done in looking solely at the rate. That is why you will see more and different rate reductions than shown on the chart for maximum rate reductions.

For example in 1968, 1969 and 1970 there were surcharges of 7.5%,

10% and 2.5%, respectively, added to the calculated tax. Thus, even though the maximum rate remained constant at 70%, the effective rate showed an increase in 1968 and 1969 reflecting the 7.5% and 10% surcharge, but a decrease in 1970 as the surcharge declined from 10% to 2.5% and then again in 1971 as the surcharge was eliminated. On the other hand, even though a surcharge was imposed in 1988, 1989 and 1990—the lesser of 5% of the calculated tax or the amount of exemptions—it had only minimal effect on the decrease in the effective tax rate.

Except for an anomaly in 1991 the trend of employment changes related to decreases and increases in effective rates is the same for both taxable incomes of $1,000,000 and $250,000. A function of the change in bracket structure, this 1991 anomaly saw the effective tax rate at $1,000,000 increase while fall at $250,000. Aside from causing a shaking of the head in disbelief about the Rube Goldberg nature of our tax system, *it does not change the results, which once again point to greater increases in employment when rates increased than when they decreased.* Using the $1,000,000 chart (Exhibit 12), and treating the 1991 tax increase as the increase it was intended to be, reveals an average increase of 1,752,000 jobs over 4 years when effective rates increased, but 1,455,000 jobs over 15 years when effective rates were reduced.

On the other hand, as displayed in Exhibit 14, in the 22 years when adjustments for inflation were reflected one way or another in the tax structure for taxable income of $1,000,000, the average effective rate change (decrease) was 0.1% to 0.2%, but the average employment increase was 1,504,000 jobs. So to put that in perspective, on average 49,000 more jobs were created annually as a result of minor inflation adjustments than by decreases in the tax rate or other bracket changes.

While the summarization of inflation adjustments on the effective tax rate for taxable income of $250,000 as reflected in Exhibit 15 is somewhat different than shown for taxable income of $1,000,000, the end result is exactly the same. With only modest inflation adjustments of 0.1 % and 0.2%, the number of jobs created exceeds those created by decreases in the tax rate or other bracket changes.

Exhibit 15

| | | | Change in Effective Income Tax Rate | Employment (thousands) | | |
|---|---|---|---|---|---|---|
| | | Effective | | | | |
| | Maximum | Income | Effective | | | |
| | Income | Tax Rate | Income | Increase | | |
| Years | Tax Rate | $250,000 | Tax Rate | (Decrease) | Increase | Decrease |
| 8 | 30.6% | 21.6% | -0.2% | 292 | 1,279 | (987) |
| 10 | 36.4% | 29.3% | -0.2% | 1,814 | 19,282 | (1,141) |
| 4 | 25.0% | 21.1% | -0.1% | 1,163 | 4,651 | 0 |
| | | | Total | 33,098 | 42,136 | (9,038) |
| | | | Average | 1,504 | 1,915 | (411) |

**Change in Effective Income Tax Rates - $250,000 Taxable Income**
**Result of Inflation Adjustments 1953-2011**
**Comparison to Employment Increases (Decreases)**

See Appendix A 8.6

Exhibit 16

| | Average Maximum Income Tax Rate | Effective Tax Rate $1,000,000 Taxable Income | Employment (thousands) | | |
|---|---|---|---|---|---|
| Years | | | Increase (Decrease) | Increase | Decrease |
| 9 | 70.0% | 67.0% | 15,111 | 16,039 | (928) |
| 9 | 91.1% | 86.4% | 2,998 | 5,107 | (2,109) |
| | | Total | 18,109 | 21,146 | (3,037) |
| | | Average | 1,006 | 1,175 | (169) |

**No Change in Effective Income Tax Rates 1953-2011**
**Based on $1,000,000 Taxable Income**
**Comparison to Employment Increases (Decreases)**

See Appendix A 6.7

The results of employment changes when there are no changes in effective rates are similar for $1,000,000 taxable income (Exhibit 16) and $250,000 taxable income (Exhibit 17) with both covering an 18-year period in which average employment increased by 1,006,000 jobs.

However, as shown in Exhibit 7, there were 48 years in which no changes were made to maximum rates, 40 resulting in an increase in employment averaging 1,973,000 jobs annually and 8 with a decrease averaging 1,542,000 jobs annually. Overall there was a net increase of

1,387,000 jobs annually when maximum tax rates were not changed.

What these statistics confirm is that looking at maximum rates alone provides an incomplete picture when relating them to employment. If $250,000 is to be considered the base amount at which individuals invest in new businesses (and thus create jobs), effective tax rates are a good measure to correlate with employment increases and decreases. But to reiterate, taxable income, at best, is only indicative of an individual's total or adjusted gross income since it reflects a series of deductions, exemptions, inclusions and exclusions that have been in almost constant change over much of these 59 years.

Exhibit 17

| No Change in Effective Income Tax Rates 1953-2011 Based on $250,000 Taxable Income Comparison to Employment Increases (Decreases) | | | | | |
|---|---|---|---|---|---|
| Years | Maximum Income Tax Rate | Effective Tax Rate $250,000 Taxable Income | Employment (thousands) | | |
| | | | Increase (Decrease) | Increase | Decrease |
| 9 | 70.0% | 67.0% | 15,111 | 16,039 | (928) |
| 9 | 91.1% | 86.4% | 2,998 | 5,107 | (2,109) |
| | | Total | 18,109 | 21,146 | (3,037) |
| | | Average | 1,006 | 1,175 | (169) |
| See Appendix A 8.7 | | | | | |

But there could be other factors that we have not yet addressed that are behind employment increases that don't necessarily relate directly to these tax rates, specifically Capital Gains Rates and Corporate Income Tax Rates.

# 8

# CAPITAL GAINS RATES
# AND EMPLOYMENT INCREASES AND DECREASES

When looking at Exhibit 18 displaying Capital Gains Rates and the related changes in employment, the results are, frankly, very surprising. One might expect that lower rates would stimulate capital investment, which in turn would create new jobs. But the facts reveal a different story.

Exhibit 18

| | | Employment Increase (Decrease) | |
|---|---|---|---|
| | Average Capital Gains | Total | Average |
| Years | Tax Rate | (thousands) | (thousands) |
| 9 | 15.0% | 4,220 | 469 |
| 8 | 20.0% | 12,119 | 1,515 |
| 16 | 24.9% | 12,837 | 802 |
| 15 | 27.9% | 26,628 | 1,775 |
| 4 | 33.2% | 7,244 | 1,811 |
| 7 | 37.8% | 16,989 | 2,427 |
| | Total | 80,037 | 1,357 |

Capital Gains Tax Rates
Comparison to Employment Increases (Decreases)
1953 - 2011

See Appendices A 9.1 to A 9.4

In the 9 years in which Capital Gains Rates were the lowest (15%), so were the average annual increases in employment (469,000 jobs). Now it is true that this period includes the recent recession in which 4,210,000 jobs were lost in 2008 and 3,687.000 jobs in 2009, or a total of 7,897,000 jobs. However, even excluding those 2 years and taking into account only the other 7 years in which the Capital Gains Rate was 15%, then the total amount of jobs created was 12,117,000 or an average annual increase of 1,731,000 jobs.

That is still below the average annual increase in jobs created when rates ranged from 27.9% to 37.8%. In fact the greatest single annual increase in jobs occurred in 1977 when the rate was 39.9%, the highest it's been in this 59-year period. And the largest average annual increase of 2,427,000 jobs occurred when rates ranged from 36.5% to 39.9% and averaged 37.8%.

*So as we saw with maximum tax rates and effective tax rates at $1,000,000 and $250,000 taxable income levels, lower capital gains rates have not produced more jobs than those created when such rates were higher, even more than twice as high.*

Thus the argument that lower taxes on individual income produce more jobs than related higher rates cannot be supported by the results for Capital Gains Rates. But there is still one more avenue to explore and that is corporate income tax rates.

# 9

# CORPORATE INCOME TAX RATES
# AND EMPLOYMENT INCREASES AND DECREASES

When discussing the top marginal tax rates for corporations over this 59-year period, one enters a morass of changing top bracket amounts, intermediate brackets that in some cases bear higher rates than the top bracket, and all of which are intermixed with changing rates. While complexity found its way into the tax rate structure for individuals, it never reached anything close to this level.

Exhibit 19

**Extract from 2011 Corporate Tax Rate Schedule**

If taxable income (line 30, Form 1120) on page 1 is:

| Over — | But not over— | Tax is: | | | Of the amount over— |
|---|---|---|---|---|---|
| $0 | $50,000 | | | 15% | $0 |
| 50,000 | 75,000 | 7,500 | + | 25% | 50,000 |
| 75,000 | 100,000 | 13,750 | + | 34% | 75,000 |
| 100,000 | 335,000 | 22,250 | + | 39% | 100,000 |
| 335,000 | 10,000,000 | 113,900 | + | 34% | 335,000 |
| 10,000,000 | 15,000,000 | 3,400,000 | + | 35% | 10,000,000 |
| 15,000,000 | 18,333,333 | 5,150,000 | + | 38% | 15,000,000 |
| 18,333,333 | ----- | | | 35% | 0 |

Source: IRS Tax Rate Schedule 2011 Instructions for Form 1120

For example, the top corporate taxable income bracket has risen from a low of $25,000 with a 52% marginal tax rate in 1953 to a high of $18,333,333 with a top marginal rate of 35% in 2011. However the 2011 rates as shown in Exhibit 19, an extract from the IRS tax rate schedule in the 2011 instructions for Form 1120 (corporate income tax return) demonstrate the strange complex provisions for different levels of taxable income.

This type of tax rate structure, though not with the same brackets or rates, existed for about half of the 59 years reviewed, which raises the question as to what constitutes the highest marginal rate. For simplification the highest rate on the last or highest level of taxable income has been used. Given the relatively narrow range of rates at these brackets—5% in 2011—I don't believe this distorts the results.

Exhibit 20

| Corporate Income Tax Top Marginal Rates 1953 - 2011 | | | | | |
|---|---|---|---|---|---|
| Comparison to Employment Increases and Decreases | | | | | |
| | Corporate | Employment | | | |
| | Income Tax Top Marginal | Average | Net | Total | |
| Years | Rate | Increase (thousands) | Increase (thousands) | Increase (thousands) | Decrease (thousands) |
| 24 | 34.8% | 1,151 | 27,621 | 38,736 | (11,115) |
| 21 | 46.9% | 1,902 | 39,939 | 41,661 | (1,722) |
| 14 | 52.0% | 891 | 12,477 | 14,586 | (2,109) |
| | Total | 1,357 | 80,037 | 94,983 | (14,946) |
| See Appendices A 10.1 to A 10.4 | | | | | |

Exhibit 20 summarizes the average corporate income tax top marginal rates and related employment increases and decreases for the 59 year period. It is clear the highest rates, which averaged 52% for 14 years, were the worst in creating jobs, averaging 891,000 annually, while the lowest rates averaging 34.8% annually over 24 years created almost 30% more jobs, averaging 1,151,000 annually. Of course this includes the 2 recession years of 2008 and 2009. Excluding those years and their 7,897,000 lost jobs from the mix brings the total jobs created to 35,518,000 and the average number of jobs created annually to 1,614,000. But, we cannot exclude a historical fact— these jobs were lost.

Even if we did, *it was the rates averaging 46.9% annually that equate to the greatest increase in jobs, averaging 1,902,000 annually over 21 years, more than twice as much as the highest rates and 65% more than the lowest rates.* This conclusion adds more information to the question whether low tax rates correlate with greater job creation.

Today there are some who contend that corporate tax rates are too high compared to other countries and need to be lowered to create more jobs domestically, yet we have seen that as with individual tax rates, more jobs have been created when rates were higher than lower. As for the rate comparison, recent studies have shown that despite the higher structural rates, the average effective tax rate was actually lower. Citizens for Tax Justice issued a report in April 2012 and reported that it had "recently examined 280 Fortune 500 companies that were profitable each year from 2008 to 2010 and found that their effective tax rate was just 18.5% over that three year period." It also found that 30 of the corporations paid no federal income tax during that time. One company, General Electric, was found to have had an effective tax rate of 2.3% for the 10 years 2002 to 2011.

A different report prepared by the Congressional Research Service in March 2011 compared the 2008 effective tax rate in the United States with the weighted average effective tax rate of the Organization for Economic Co-operation and Development (OECD) excluding the United States and found the U.S. rate to be 27.1% while the OECD rate was 27.7%.

That does not mean the U.S. rate is among the lowest. In its report, *Paying Taxes 2012, The Global Picture,* PricewaterhouseCoopers found that among 183 countries the U.S. tax rate on profit was 27.6%, which was in the same range as Japan (27.0%) and Australia (26.0%), above the United Kingdom (23.1%), Mexico (24.5%), Italy (22.8%), India (24.6%), Germany (19.0%) and Brazil (22.4%), and well above Canada (9.4%), and Spain (1.2%). However, when including labor and other taxes, except for Canada (28.8%), the United Kingdom (37.3%) and Spain (38.7%), the U.S. total tax rate of 46.7% was equal to Germany (46.7%), but below all the others listed: China (63.5%), France (65.7%), Italy (68.5%), Brazil (67.1%), India (61.8%), Mexico (52.7%), Australia (47.7%) and Russia (46.9%). All of which suggests that on a global basis corporate income tax is but one of other taxes and costs to consider when evaluating investment options.

Before addressing this issue further and coming to a conclusion, let's digress a moment to look at job creation during each of the presidencies of the last 59 years. This has a certain relevance to our subject as some former presidents are known to have been philosophically committed to lower taxes and it will be informative to see whether their philosophies were put into action and, if so, to what extent they affected job creation.

# 10

# THE PRESIDENTS 1953-2011
## TAX RATES
## AND EMPLOYMENT INCREASES AND DECREASES

Exhibit 21 summarizes the presidencies of Dwight Eisenhower in 1953 to the end of Barack Obama's third year in office in 2011. Before relating employment to each presidency, though, let's first look at the tax rate structure and tax rates that changed in their respective terms, using taxable income of $250,000 as the basis for comparison. Details supporting the following comments can be found in Appendices B 5.1 and B 5.2.

Under Eisenhower the Maximum Tax Rate dropped from 92% to 91% and the top rate on $250,000 taxable income dropped from 92% to 89%. More significantly, the top bracket, over which the maximum rate applied, was raised to $400,000 from $200,000. This meant that an individual who had taxable income of $250,000 in 1953, paid a tax of $206,716, but in 1960, the last year of the Eisenhower presidency, paid $179,140, a decrease of $27,576 or 13.3%.

The subsequent presidencies of John Kennedy and Lyndon Johnson saw rates fall even further. Both the maximum rate and the rate on taxable income of $250,000 fell to a low of 70%, which lasted into the Richard Nixon presidency in 1969. In 1967 an individual with taxable income of $250,000 paid a tax of $145,980, a decrease of $33,160, or 18.5%% from the last Eisenhower year. Other than a surcharge with varying rate impacts in 1968, 1969 and 1970, tax brackets and rates held steady throughout the Nixon and Gerald Ford presidencies.

During the Jimmy Carter presidency, while the maximum rate held steady at 70%, the top bracket, over which the maximum rate applied, was raised first from $200,000 to $202,300 and then to $215,400. The net effect was a decrease of $4,256 to $141,724 in 1980, or 2.9% in the tax paid on $250,0000 taxable income.

In 1981 Ronald Reagan became president and a year later began a string of the largest decreases in both tax bracket and rate structures in these 59 years. The maximum rate dropped from 70% to 50%, to 38.5% and then 28% in 1988, the last year of his presidency, while the top bracket was reduced from $215,400 in 1981 to $149,250 in 1988 with several bracket changes in the years in between. The impact of these changes can be seen in the tax on $250,000 taxable income, which went from $141,724 in 1980 to $71,092 in 1988, a decrease of $70,632, or 49.8%. And though there was a surcharge of 5% in 1988, 1989 and 1990, the manner in which it was calculated had only a de minimis effect on the total tax.

The low 28% rate lasted for 2 years into the George H. W. Bush (1) presidency but was raised to 31% in 1991; however, because the top bracket (and consequently the $250,000 bracket) changed to $82,150 and then $86,500, the amount of tax actually paid at the $250,000 income level continued to decrease and reached $70,251, which up to that point in time, was a 40 year low.

In Bill Clinton's first year in 1993, the top rate rose to 39.6%, an increase of 8.6 percentage points, and the top bracket rose to $250,000 but because that rate was applied to income *above* $250,000, that amount ($250,000) was subject to a 36% rate—result: the tax increased $5,278 to $75,529, or 7.5%. Although the 39.6% rate held steady throughout the remainder of Clinton's term, inflation adjustments lowered the tax paid on $250,000 taxable income to $73,049 in 2000, the last year of his presidency.

Shortly after George W. Bush (2) entered office in 2001, tax rates were lowered and tax brackets increased, the latter having the effect of further lowering the amount of tax paid. First the top rates were reduced from 39.6% to 39.1%, 38.6% and finally to 35.0%, which is where it remains at this time. The rate at which $250,000 taxable income was taxed was lowered from 36% in 2000 to 35.5%, 35%, and then to 33% where it remains today.

That brought the tax on $250,000 taxable income in Bush (2)'s last year in office to $61,229 a decease of $11,820, or 16.2% (including inflation adjustments) from Clinton's last year in office.

While the rates have remained the same in the Barack Obama administration, inflation adjustments continue to lower the actual amount of tax paid so that $59,955 was the tax paid on $250,000 taxable income in 2011, an amount that represents the lowest tax paid on that level of income in the 59 years of this study, not to mention the many years before.

Now let's look at employment for each of these presidential terms summarized in Exhibit 21.

Exhibit 21

| Average Maximum Individual Tax Rates by Presidential Term 1953-2011 | | | | | | |
|---|---|---|---|---|---|---|
| Comparison to Average, Total, Best, and Worst Employment Increases (Decreases) | | | | | | |
| | Years in Office | Average Maximum Income Tax Rates | Employment Increase (Decrease) (In thousands) | | | |
| President and Term | | | Average | Total | Best | Worst |
| Eisenhower: Jan, 1953 - Jan, 1961 | 8 | 91.1% | 522 | 4,176 | 3,000 | (1,576) |
| Kennedy/Johnson: Jan, 1961- Jan, 1965 | 4 | 87.5% | 1,055 | 4,221 | 1,670 | 332 |
| Johnson: Jan, 1965- Jan, 1969 | 4 | 70.0% | 1,702 | 6,808 | 2,201 | 1,029 |
| Nixon/Ford: Jan, 1969 - Jan, 1977 | 8 | 70.0% | 1,640 | 13,123 | 3,394 | (928) |
| Carter: Jan, 1977 - Jan. 1981 | 4 | 70.0% | 2,507 | 10,027 | 4,456 | 76 |
| Reagan: Jan, 1981 - Jan, 1989 | 8 | 48.3% | 2,094 | 16,753 | 4,040 | (531) |
| Bush (1): Jan, 1989 - Jan, 1993 | 4 | 29.5% | 592 | 2,367 | 2,373 | (1,141) |
| Clinton: Jan, 1993 - Jan, 2001 | 8 | 39.6% | 2,338 | 18,703 | 3,173 | 462 |
| Bush (2): Jan, 2001 - Jan, 2009 | 8 | 36.0% | 551 | 4,409 | 2,905 | (4,210) |
| Obama: Jan, 2009 - | 3 | 35.0% | (183) | (550) | 2,307 | (3,687) |
| See Appendices A 11.1 and A 11.2 | | | | | | |
| (Beginning January of year entering office and ending January of year leaving office) | | | | | | |

What strikes you immediately are the highlighted numbers showing the best (and worst) changes in employment: best average annual increase—Carter; best total increase—Clinton; best single year increase—Carter; worst single year decrease—Bush (2). Aside from what you think about their respective presidential terms, these results relate to the tax rates and policies then in effect. To the extent they (and the respective Congress in session) influenced or created them is not the issue though to a certain degree there is a general awareness that tax reductions were principal objectives of Reagan and George W. Bush (2) while Clinton and George H. W. Bush (1) found it necessary to effect tax increases. However as noted previously, even though Bush (1) raised the maximum tax rate from 28% to 31%, individuals earning $250,000 actually paid less tax in the last year of his administration (1992) than in the last year of the Reagan administration (1988).

Putting that aside, when we focus on tax rates and employment changes we find the same pattern elicited earlier. Namely **the lowest rates produced significantly less jobs than did the higher rates.** Taking the 3 lowest rates together—29.5%, 35% and 36%— over a period of 15 years, a net total of 6,226,000 jobs were created. Compare that to the 2 highest rates—91.1% and 87.5%—over 12 years when 8,397,000 jobs were created. To summarize it differently, during the years of the 3 lowest rates, an average of 415,000 jobs were created each year (6,226,000/15), but in the years when the highest rates were in effect, the average annual increase was 700,000 jobs (8,397,000/12). Looking at the average increase per year when rates were at least 39.6% and no higher than 70%, the comparison is even more vivid. The least average number of jobs created during all of the above presidencies when rates fell within that range, was 1,640,000 (Nixon/Ford) and the largest average annual increase was 2,507,000 (Carter).

Perhaps some readers with specific opinions of our presidents find it difficult to accept the above conclusions and would argue that the results would be different if the employment changes attributed to each president began one year after assuming office and ended one year after leaving office. So to eliminate any controversy on this point and demonstrate that though that analysis does change the historical record of a president's performance, it does not change the fundamental conclusion of this analysis that more jobs were created when maximum income tax rates were higher rather than lower.

Exhibit 22 summarizes each president's performance on that basis and immediately presents significant differences with the previous analysis.

Notably, we see the largest total increase in employment is attributable to Reagan with 19,389, 000 jobs followed by Nixon/Ford (15,604,000) and then Clinton (13,735,000), with the average annual increase following in that same order. The smallest numbers of jobs created over 8 years sees a change as Bush (2) takes that place with a low of 2,799,000 jobs and all other 8 year presidencies registering an increase of at least 6,000.000 jobs.

Exhibit 22

| Average Maximum Individual Tax Rates by Presidential Term 1953-2011 | | | | |
|---|---|---|---|---|
| Comparison to Average and Total Employment Increases (Decreases) | | | | |
| President and Term | Years in Office | Average Maximum Income Tax Rates * | Employment* Increase (Decrease) (In thousands) | |
| | | | Average | Total |
| Eisenhower: Jan, 1953 - Jan, 1961 | 8 | 91.1% | 761 | 6,084 |
| Kennedy/Johnson: Jan, 1961- Jan, 1965 | 4 | 87.5% | 1,523 | 6,090 |
| Johnson: Jan, 1965- Jan, 1969 | 4 | 70.0% | 1,646 | 6,582 |
| Nixon/Ford: Jan, 1969 - Jan, 1977 | 8 | 70.0% | 1,951 | 15,604 |
| Carter: Jan, 1977 - Jan. 1981 | 4 | 70.0% | 1,327 | 5,308 |
| Reagan: Jan, 1981 - Jan, 1989 | 8 | 48.3% | 2,424 | 19,389 |
| Bush (1): Jan, 1989 - Jan, 1993 | 4 | 29.5% | 721 | 2,885 |
| Clinton: Jan, 1993 - Jan, 2001 | 8 | 39.6% | 1,717 | 13,735 |
| Bush (2): Jan, 2001 - Jan, 2009 | 8 | 36.0% | 350 | 2,799 |
| Obama: Jan, 2009 - | 2 | 35.0% | 1,569 | 3,137 |

See Appendices A 12.1 and A 12.2

\* Beginning January one year after entering office and ending January one year after leaving office.

Looking at the average number of jobs puts presidential performance in even sharper focus with Bush (2) showing the least number of jobs created with an average annual increase of 350,000 jobs followed by Bush (1), 721,000 jobs and Eisenhower, 761,000 jobs.

This latter analysis might make some Republicans or Democrats feel better in the elevation or downgrading of a president's performance, and though it changes some of the numbers (employment and tax rates), it does not change the conclusion as to the impact of income tax rates on employment.

During a period of 14 years with the three lowest tax rates—29.5%, 36.0% and 35%—8,821,000 jobs were created, or an average of 630,000 jobs annually. That compares with a total of 12,174,000 jobs created during 12 years of the highest tax rates—91.1% and 87.5%—or an average of 1,014,000 jobs annually and when rates were at least 39.6% and no higher than 70%, during the remaining 32* years, 60,618,000 jobs were created, or an average annual increase of 1,894,000 jobs, confirming the earlier conclusion that *the lowest rates produced significantly less jobs than did the higher rates.*

* Since only 2 years are attributed to Obama, his first having been attributed to Bush (1), only 58 years of results are included.

# 11

# WHAT DOES ALL THIS MEAN?

With this last analysis we have again confirmed what was apparent earlier: *there has been no direct correlation between lower tax rates and job creation.* Indeed if any conclusion can be drawn it is that higher rates have historically created more jobs than lower rates. Yes, one can argue accurately that when rates were reduced, there was an upsurge in jobs created as occurred during the Reagan administration when the maximum rates were reduced from 70% to 50% to 28%. And reinforce that argument with the fact that there was a sharp decrease in jobs created when rates were increased from 28% to 31% during the George H. W. Bush (1) administration. But then one can argue with equal accuracy that there was an even greater surge in jobs created when rates were increased as occurred during the Clinton administration. And one can reinforce that argument with the fact that there was an even sharper decrease in jobs created after the maximum rates were reduced during the George W. Bush (2) administration from 39.6% to 35%, a reduction that has carried into the Obama administration.

As a footnote for those who believe current tax rates are too high. I offer Exhibit 22, a listing of what the 2011 taxes at current rates for taxable income of $250,000 would be deflated to then current dollars for each of every five years from 2010 back to 1955 compared to the actual tax in those years.

Previously we saw that the effective rate today is the lowest it's been in the 59 years of this study, but we can now see what that means in absolute amounts. The 2011 tax of $59,955 is equivalent to $8,783 in current 1955 dollars when the actual tax then was $179,140, or in other words, we are now paying 95.1% less in taxes than was paid then. While the differential between today's rates and those of the mid 1980's and 1990's is not as great as in earlier years, it is still substantial. And those higher rates were where we saw some of the largest increases in employment.

Exhibit 23

| | Bracket Rate At or Before $250,000 | Effective Tax rate | Tax in Current Dollars | 2011 Tax in Deflated Current Dollars | Percentage Decrease in Current Taxes |
|---|---|---|---|---|---|
| **2011 Taxes Based on $250,000 Taxable Income** | | | | | |
| **Deflated to Current Dollars in Selected Years** | | | | | |
| **1955-2010** | | | | | |
| Year | | | | | |
| 1955 | 89.00% | 71.66% | $179,140 | $8,783 | 95.10% |
| 1960 | 89.00% | 71.66% | $179,140 | $9,847 | 94.50% |
| 1965 | 70.00% | 58.39% | $145,980 | $10,547 | 92.78% |
| 1970 | 70.00% | 59.85% | $149,630 | $12,876 | 91.39% |
| 1975 | 70.00% | 58.39% | $145,980 | $17,771 | 87.83% |
| 1980 | 70.00% | 56.69% | $141,724 | $25,284 | 82.16% |
| 1985 | 50.00% | 42.26% | $104,928 | $32,604 | 68.93% |
| 1990 | 28.00% | 28.46% | $71,148 | $38,230 | 46.27% |
| 1995 | 36.00% | 29.97% | $74,923 | $43,173 | 42.38% |
| 2000 | 36.00% | 29.22% | $73,049 | $46,938 | 35.74% |
| 2005 | 33.00% | 25.24% | $63,092 | $52,904 | 16.15% |
| 2010 | 33.00% | 24.11% | $60,282 | $58,720 | 2.59% |
| 2011 | 33.00% | 23.98% | $59,955 | $59,955 | - |
| See Appendix A 12 | | | | | |

*So to repeat, the only conclusion one can draw from a review of historical facts is that there has been no correlation between low tax rates and job creation over the last 59 years.* Those who disagree with that conclusion have the burden of explaining why the current situation will be any different than the historical record—or actual results—of prior years.

# 12

# AN OPINION

Up to now I have attempted to accumulate historical data in as objective a manner as possible to reach an unbiased conclusion. I believe I have done that and welcome all objective as opposed to ideological criticism as to the data used, the manner of its accumulation or the conclusion reached.

Now, however, I would like to offer an opinion as to why the historical results are what they are and then look at the situation today to see if there are any similarities with the past that might help chart a path out of this unacceptable condition of low job growth and high unemployment.

First, let's focus on tax rates. To suggest that the taxes individuals pay have no bearing on investment decisions is naive and inaccurate. Of course taxes matter. But they matter in different ways to individuals starting a new or expanding an existing business or to established multinational corporations.

Let's take the individual starting a new business. I doubt that his first thought—and I use the masculine form to include the feminine—is what tax will I pay if my business is successful. No, he has an idea that he believes is unique or has a point of difference with an existing product or service that will allow him to create a successful business. For example, Ben and Jerry's was opened in 1978 by its founders, Ben Cohen and Jerry Greenfield, who had an idea about making ice cream they believed unique. That was during the Carter administration when the maximum tax rate was 70%.

Jeff Bezos, Amazon.com's founder incorporated his business in 1994 and went online in 1995. Google began with a search engine created by Larry Page and Sergey Brin at Stanford in 1996, received its first infusion of outside capital ($100,000) in 1998 and its second ($25,000,000 in 1999). Both companies were created during the Clinton administration when the maximum tax rate was 39.6%, and they have been expanding ever since.

Howard Schultz founded a company, Il Giornale in 1986 during the Reagan administration when the tax rate was 50% and a year later when the maximum tax rate was 38.5%, acquired the assets of Starbucks, his former employer, and began opening new stores.

I find it hard to believe that the founders of or investors in any of these ventures allowed the then existing tax rates to be a determining factor in whether to make an investment. I'm sure the fundamental question they addressed was whether the product or service was unique or different enough to produce the required demand and the overall cost structure would allow the business to become profitable. Indeed in its earlier years when a business is just starting, losses are more likely than profits, and it may be possible for individuals to use such losses as offsets to other income or other profitable ventures. In such instances the higher tax rates are actually beneficial as it means the government will absorb a greater percentage of the loss.

On the other hand as the business grows and particularly when it becomes a global operation, taxes become a more important consideration, as do overall operating costs. It is routine for companies to shift profits from high tax rate countries to lower tax rate countries by establishing its headquarters in countries with favorable tax laws, or more broadly, by using transfer pricing techniques in countries with low rates. Simplistically that means having one subsidiary manufacturing a product in a low cost country, but then charging a higher price to another subsidiary in a high tax country, thereby increasing that high tax subsidiary's costs and reducing its profits. Keeping all or the majority of research and development, marketing and other costs that benefit global operations in the subsidiary in the high tax country can accomplish the same result. These are but some of the ways that multinational companies reduce their taxes, but keep in mind that when evaluating whether to expand an existing facility or create a new one in a different country, tax rates are only one consideration.

In any event, one must ask the question if lowering the tax rate would induce multi-national companies to invest more in the United States, to which I would answer in the negative. Aside from those who believe that if the U.S. lowered its tax rate, other countries would follow suit, resulting in no new jobs and even lower tax revenues, I believe the driving force to invest elsewhere is not just taxes, but the overall cost structure including taxes in such countries, and that is not about to change. Will lower taxes prompt companies to stop opening or expanding call centers overseas or stop manufacturing products in China? I don't think so.

If it isn't low tax rates, then what is it that prompts an individual or corporation to invest in or expand a business? First and foremost is the belief that there is or will be a demand for the product or service and that it can be created and delivered at a profit. In a difficult economy investments are made when these conditions exist, but even in a booming economy, they will not be made in their absence. Now granted, one may be more willing to take a chance or make a bigger investment when the economy is expanding than when it is stagnant, but in the final analysis it is the potential of the product or service that is the driving force.

With that being said, let's look at what is, in my view, the overriding conditions that must be present to induce investments on a scale large enough to power the economy out of its doldrums and put people back to work. *That condition is confidence, and how we develop that confidence is truly the issue we face today.*

Building confidence begins with the President and Congress who must demonstrate that they are working together toward a common goal, which clearly is not, nor has been the case, at least in the recent past.

There must be a certainty about the tax, environmental, regulatory and other laws and policies that will be in effect in the coming years. These cannot be unknown, moving or ever-changing targets. Successful businessmen, by definition, are not stupid. They can plan for and deal with a multitude of conditions provided they know what they are.

There must be an acknowledgement that regulations are necessary, particularly to monitor those businesses that have grossly abused the public trust and contributed heavily to the deleterious condition in which we find the economy today. On the other hand there must be a balance so that businesses are not over-regulated and initiative is stifled.

The Administration and Congress must simultaneously address the issues of stimulus through infrastructure investment and deficit reduction with such actions incorporating both spending cuts and higher taxes, recognizing that one without the other is a recipe for disaster.

There must be recognition that funding for both Medicare and Social Security must be addressed today to assure adequate resources for future beneficiaries or both programs must be dramatically altered and their benefits reduced.

Longer term, we must seriously address a revision of the tax code with the objective of greatly reducing its complexity and increasing its fairness through elimination of the many tax avoidance schemes that enable individuals and corporations to pay a lesser tax rate then otherwise envisioned.

Finally, politicians of every stripe must first recognize that the world is not black or white, but many shades of gray, and then take off their ideological blinders to look for realistic solutions to the problems confronting the country while abandoning politics as usual, a term perhaps best described by the very late Groucho Marx:

"Politics is the art of looking for trouble, finding it everywhere, diagnosing it incorrectly and applying the wrong remedies."

# APPENDICES

Maximum Income Tax Rates 1953-2011
Comparison to Employment increases (Decreases)
Sorted by Year

| Year | Maximum Income Tax Rate (1) | Employment Increase (Decrease) (2) (thousands) | Year | Maximum Income Tax Rate (1) | Employment Increase (Decrease) (2) (thousands) |
|---|---|---|---|---|---|
| 1953 | 92.0% | (1,576) | 1983 | 50.0% | 4,040 |
| 1954 | 91.0% | 729 | 1984 | 50.0% | 3,101 |
| 1955 | 91.0% | 3,000 | 1985 | 50.0% | 2,585 |
| 1956 | 91.0% | (121) | 1986 | 50.0% | 2,066 |
| 1957 | 91.0% | (412) | 1987 | 38.5% | 3,063 |
| 1958 | 91.0% | 648 | 1988* | 28.0% | 2,692 |
| 1959 | 91.0% | 1,479 | 1989* | 28.0% | 2,373 |
| 1960 | 91.0% | 429 | 1990* | 28.0% | (1,141) |
| 1961 | 91.0% | 332 | 1991 | 31.0% | 38 |
| 1962 | 91.0% | 964 | 1992 | 31.0% | 1,097 |
| 1963 | 91.0% | 1,255 | 1993 | 39.6% | 2,891 |
| 1964 | 77.0% | 1,670 | 1994 | 39.6% | 2,697 |
| 1965 | 70.0% | 2,201 | 1995 | 39.6% | 462 |
| 1966 | 70.0% | 1,473 | 1996 | 39.6% | 3,173 |
| 1967 | 70.0% | 1,029 | 1997 | 39.6% | 2,428 |
| 1968* | 70.0% | 2,105 | 1998 | 39.6% | 2,301 |
| 1969* | 70.0% | 1,975 | 1999 | 39.6% | 3,532 |
| 1970* | 70.0% | 84 | 2000 | 39.6% | 1,219 |
| 1971 | 70.0% | 2,095 | 2001 | 39.1% | (2,077) |
| 1972 | 70.0% | 2,202 | 2002 | 38.6% | 1,716 |
| 1973 | 70.0% | 3,394 | 2003 | 35.0% | 1,055 |
| 1974 | 70.0% | (928) | 2004 | 35.0% | 1,773 |
| 1975 | 70.0% | 1,773 | 2005 | 35.0% | 2,905 |
| 1976 | 70.0% | 2,528 | 2006 | 35.0% | 2,878 |
| 1977 | 70.0% | 4,456 | 2007 | 35.0% | 369 |
| 1978 | 70.0% | 3,564 | 2008 | 35.0% | (4,210) |
| 1979 | 70.0% | 1,931 | 2009 | 35.0% | (3,687) |
| 1980 | 70.0% | 76 | 2010 | 35.0% | 830 |
| 1981* | 70.0% | (263) | 2011 | 35.0% | 2,307 |
| 1982 | 50.0% | (531) | | | |

(1) See Appendix B-1.1    (2) See Appendix C-1.1
*Does not reflect imposition or removal of surcharge or credit

Maximum Income Tax Rates 1953-2011
Comparison to Employment Increases (Decreases)
Sorted by Tax Rate

| Year | Maximum Income Tax Rate (1) | Employment Increase (Decrease) (2) (thousands) | Year | Maximum Income Tax Rate (1) | Employment Increase (Decrease) (2) (thousands) |
|---|---|---|---|---|---|
| 1988* | 28.0% | 2,692 | 1965 | 70.0% | 2,201 |
| 1989* | 28.0% | 2,373 | 1966 | 70.0% | 1,473 |
| 1990* | 28.0% | (1,141) | 1967 | 70.0% | 1,029 |
| 1991 | 31.0% | 38 | 1968* | 70.0% | 2,105 |
| 1992 | 31.0% | 1,097 | 1969* | 70.0% | 1,975 |
| 5 | 29.2% | 1,012 | 1970* | 70.0% | 84 |
| 2003 | 35.0% | 1,055 | 1971 | 70.0% | 2,095 |
| 2004 | 35.0% | 1,773 | 1972 | 70.0% | 2,202 |
| 2005 | 35.0% | 2,905 | 1973 | 70.0% | 3,394 |
| 2006 | 35.0% | 2,878 | 1974 | 70.0% | (928) |
| 2007 | 35.0% | 369 | 1975 | 70.0% | 1,773 |
| 2008 | 35.0% | (4,210) | 1976 | 70.0% | 2,528 |
| 2009 | 35.0% | (3,687) | 1977 | 70.0% | 4,456 |
| 2010 | 35.0% | 830 | 1978 | 70.0% | 3,564 |
| 2011 | 35.0% | 2,307 | 1979 | 70.0% | 1,931 |
| 9 | 35.0% | 469 | 1980 | 70.0% | 76 |
| 1987 | 38.5% | 3,063 | 1981* | 70.0% | (263) |
| 2002 | 38.6% | 1,716 | 1964 | 77.0% | 1,670 |
| 2001 | 39.1% | (2,077) | 18 | 70.4% | 1,743 |
| 1993 | 39.6% | 2,891 | 1954 | 91.0% | 729 |
| 1994 | 39.6% | 2,697 | 1955 | 91.0% | 3,000 |
| 1995 | 39.6% | 462 | 1956 | 91.0% | (121) |
| 1996 | 39.6% | 3,173 | 1957 | 91.0% | (412) |
| 1997 | 39.6% | 2,428 | 1958 | 91.0% | 648 |
| 1998 | 39.6% | 2,301 | 1959 | 91.0% | 1,479 |
| 1999 | 39.6% | 3,532 | 1960 | 91.0% | 429 |
| 2000 | 39.6% | 1,219 | 1961 | 91.0% | 332 |
| 11 | 39.4% | 1,946 | 1962 | 91.0% | 964 |
| 1982 | 50.0% | (531) | 1963 | 91.0% | 1,255 |
| 1983 | 50.0% | 4,040 | 1953 | 92.0% | (1,576) |
| 1984 | 50.0% | 3,101 | 11 | 91.1% | 612 |
| 1985 | 50.0% | 2,585 | | | |
| 1986 | 50.0% | 2,066 | | | |
| 5 | 50.0% | 2,252 | | | |

(1) See Appendix A-1.1    (2) See Appendix C-1.1
*Does not reflect imposition or removal of surcharge or credit

## Maximum Income Tax Rates 1953-1982
### Comparison to Employment Increases (Decreases)

| Year | Maximum Income Tax Rate (1) | Employment Increase (Decrease) (2) (thousands) | Employment | |
|------|------|------|------|------|
| | | | Increase (thousands) | Decrease (thousands) |
| 1953 | 92.00% | (1,576) | | (1,576) |
| 1954 | 91.00% | 729 | 729 | |
| 1955 | 91.00% | 3,000 | 3,000 | |
| 1956 | 91.00% | (121) | | (121) |
| 1957 | 91.00% | (412) | | (412) |
| 1958 | 91.00% | 648 | 648 | |
| 1959 | 91.00% | 1,479 | 1,479 | |
| 1960 | 91.00% | 429 | 429 | |
| 1961 | 91.00% | 332 | 332 | |
| 1962 | 91.00% | 964 | 964 | |
| 1963 | 91.00% | 1,255 | 1,255 | |
| 1964 | 77.00% | 1,670 | 1,670 | |
| 1965 | 70.00% | 2,201 | 2,201 | |
| 1966 | 70.00% | 1,473 | 1,473 | |
| 1967 | 70.00% | 1,029 | 1,029 | |
| 1968* | 70.00% | 2,105 | 2,105 | |
| 1969* | 70.00% | 1,975 | 1,975 | |
| 1970* | 70.00% | 84 | 84 | |
| 1971 | 70.00% | 2,095 | 2,095 | |
| 1972 | 70.00% | 2,202 | 2,202 | |
| 1973 | 70.00% | 3,394 | 3,394 | |
| 1974 | 70.00% | (928) | | (928) |
| 1975 | 70.00% | 1,773 | 1,773 | |
| 1976 | 70.00% | 2,528 | 2,528 | |
| 1977 | 70.00% | 4,456 | 4,456 | |
| 1978 | 70.00% | 3,564 | 3,564 | |
| 1979 | 70.00% | 1,931 | 1,931 | |
| 1980 | 70.00% | 76 | 76 | |
| 1981* | 70.00% | (263) | | (263) |
| 1982 | 50.00% | (531) | | (531) |

(1) See Appendix B-1.1
(2) See Appendix C-1.1
*Does not reflect imposition or removal of surcharge or credit

## Maximum Income Tax Rates 1983-2011
## Comparison to Employment Increases (Decreases)

| Year | Maximum Income Tax Rate (1) | Employment Increase (Decrease) (2) (thousands) | Employment | |
|---|---|---|---|---|
| | | | Increase (thousands) | Decrease (thousands) |
| 1983 | 50.00% | 4,040 | 4,040 | |
| 1984 | 50.00% | 3,101 | 3,101 | |
| 1985 | 50.00% | 2,585 | 2,585 | |
| 1986 | 50.00% | 2,066 | 2,066 | |
| 1987 | 38.50% | 3,063 | 3,063 | |
| 1988* | 28.00% | 2,692 | 2,692 | |
| 1989* | 28.00% | 2,373 | 2,373 | |
| 1990* | 28.00% | (1,141) | | (1,141) |
| 1991 | 31.00% | 38 | 38 | |
| 1992 | 31.00% | 1,097 | 1,097 | |
| 1993 | 39.60% | 2,891 | 2,891 | |
| 1994 | 39.60% | 2,697 | 2,697 | |
| 1995 | 39.60% | 462 | 462 | |
| 1996 | 39.60% | 3,173 | 3,173 | |
| 1997 | 39.60% | 2,428 | 2,428 | |
| 1998 | 39.60% | 2,301 | 2,301 | |
| 1999 | 39.60% | 3,532 | 3,532 | |
| 2000 | 39.60% | 1,219 | 1,219 | |
| 2001 | 39.10% | (2,077) | | (2,077) |
| 2002 | 38.60% | 1,716 | 1,716 | |
| 2003 | 35.00% | 1,055 | 1,055 | |
| 2004 | 35.00% | 1,773 | 1,773 | |
| 2005 | 35.00% | 2,905 | 2,905 | |
| 2006 | 35.00% | 2,878 | 2,878 | |
| 2007 | 35.00% | 369 | 369 | |
| 2008 | 35.00% | (4,210) | | (4,210) |
| 2009 | 35.00% | (3,687) | | (3,687) |
| 2010 | 35.00% | 830 | 830 | |
| 2011 | 35.00% | 2,307 | 2,307 | |

(1) See Appendix B-1.1

(2) See Appendix C-1.1

*Does not reflect imposition or removal of surcharge or credit

### Maximum Income Tax Rates 1953-2011
### Comparison to Employment Increases (Decreases)
### By Tax Rate

| Year | Maximum Tax Rate (1) | Employment Increase (Decrease) (2) (thousands) | Employment | |
|---|---|---|---|---|
| | | | Increase (thousands) | Decrease (thousands) |
| 1988* | 28.00% | 2,692 | 2,692 | |
| 1989* | 28.00% | 2,373 | 2,373 | |
| 1990* | 28.00% | (1,141) | | (1,141) |
| 1991 | 31.00% | 38 | 38 | |
| 1992 | 31.00% | 1,097 | 1,097 | |
| 5 | 29.20% | 5,059 | 6,200 | (1,141) |
| 2003 | 35.00% | 1,055 | 1,055 | |
| 2004 | 35.00% | 1,773 | 1,773 | |
| 2005 | 35.00% | 2,905 | 2,905 | |
| 2006 | 35.00% | 2,878 | 2,878 | |
| 2007 | 35.00% | 369 | 369 | |
| 2008 | 35.00% | (4,210) | | (4,210) |
| 2009 | 35.00% | (3,687) | | (3,687) |
| 2010 | 35.00% | 830 | 830 | |
| 2011 | 35.00% | 2,307 | 2,307 | |
| 9 | 35.00% | 4,220 | 12,117 | (7,897) |
| 1987 | 38.50% | 3,063 | 3,063 | |
| 2002 | 38.60% | 1,716 | 1,716 | |
| 2001 | 39.10% | (2,077) | | (2,077) |
| 1993 | 39.60% | 2,891 | 2,891 | |
| 1994 | 39.60% | 2,697 | 2,697 | |
| 1995 | 39.60% | 462 | 462 | |
| 1996 | 39.60% | 3,173 | 3,173 | |
| 1997 | 39.60% | 2,428 | 2,428 | |
| 1998 | 39.60% | 2,301 | 2,301 | |
| 1999 | 39.60% | 3,532 | 3,532 | |
| 2000 | 39.60% | 1,219 | 1,219 | |
| 11 | 39.36% | 21,405 | 23,482 | (2,077) |
| 1982 | 50.00% | (531) | | (531) |
| 1983 | 50.00% | 4,040 | 4,040 | |
| 1984 | 50.00% | 3,101 | 3,101 | |
| 1985 | 50.00% | 2,585 | 2,585 | |
| 1986 | 50.00% | 2,066 | 2,066 | |
| 5 | 50.00% | 11,261 | 11,792 | (531) |

(1) See Appendix B-1.1
(2) See Appendix C-1.1
*Does not reflect imposition or removal of surcharge or credit

### Maximum Income Tax Rates 1953-2011
### Comparison to Employment Increases (Decreases)
### By Tax Rate

| Year | Maximum Income Tax Rate (1) | Employment Increase (Decrease) (2) (thousands) | Employment | |
|------|------|------|------|------|
| | | | Increase (thousands) | Decrease (thousands) |
| 1965 | 70.00% | 2,201 | 2,201 | |
| 1966 | 70.00% | 1,473 | 1,473 | |
| 1967 | 70.00% | 1,029 | 1,029 | |
| 1968* | 70.00% | 2,105 | 2,105 | |
| 1969* | 70.00% | 1,975 | 1,975 | |
| 1970* | 70.00% | 84 | 84 | |
| 1971 | 70.00% | 2,095 | 2,095 | |
| 1972 | 70.00% | 2,202 | 2,202 | |
| 1973 | 70.00% | 3,394 | 3,394 | |
| 1974 | 70.00% | (928) | | (928) |
| 1975 | 70.00% | 1,773 | 1,773 | |
| 1976 | 70.00% | 2,528 | 2,528 | |
| 1977 | 70.00% | 4,456 | 4,456 | |
| 1978 | 70.00% | 3,564 | 3,564 | |
| 1979 | 70.00% | 1,931 | 1,931 | |
| 1980 | 70.00% | 76 | 76 | |
| 1981* | 70.00% | (263) | | (263) |
| 1964 | 77.00% | 1,670 | 1,670 | |
| 18 | 70.39% | 31,365 | 32,556 | (1,191) |
| 1954 | 91.00% | 729 | 729 | |
| 1955 | 91.00% | 3,000 | 3,000 | |
| 1956 | 91.00% | (121) | | (121) |
| 1957 | 91.00% | (412) | | (412) |
| 1958 | 91.00% | 648 | 648 | |
| 1959 | 91.00% | 1,479 | 1,479 | |
| 1960 | 91.00% | 429 | 429 | |
| 1961 | 91.00% | 332 | 332 | |
| 1962 | 91.00% | 964 | 964 | |
| 1963 | 91.00% | 1,255 | 1,255 | |
| 1953 | 92.00% | (1,576) | | (1,576) |
| 11 | 91.09% | 6,727 | 8,836 | (2,109) |

(1) See Appendix B-1.1

(2) See Appendix C-1.1

*Does not reflect imposition or removal of surcharge or credit

Changes in Maximum Income Tax Rates 1953-1982
Comparison to Employment Increases and Decreases
Sorted by Year

| Year | Change in Maximum Tax Rate (1) | Employment Increase (2) (Decrease) (thousands) | Employment Increase (Decrease) | | | | | |
|---|---|---|---|---|---|---|---|---|
| | | | Reduction in Tax Rate | | | Increase in Tax Rate | | |
| | | | Year of Change | Years Later | | Year of Change | Years Later | |
| | | | | 1 | 2 | | 1 | 2 |
| 1953 | 0.00% | (1,576) | | | | | | |
| 1954 | -1.00% | 729 | 729 | 3,000 | (121) | | | |
| 1955 | 0.00% | 3,000 | | | | | | |
| 1956 | 0.00% | (121) | | | | | | |
| 1957 | 0.00% | (412) | | | | | | |
| 1958 | 0.00% | 648 | | | | | | |
| 1959 | 0.00% | 1,479 | | | | | | |
| 1960 | 0.00% | 429 | | | | | | |
| 1961 | 0.00% | 332 | | | | | | |
| 1962 | 0.00% | 964 | | | | | | |
| 1963 | 0.00% | 1,255 | | | | | | |
| 1964 | -14.00% | 1,670 | 1,670 | 2,201 | 1,473 | | | |
| 1965 | -7.00% | 2,201 | 2,201 | 1,473 | 1,029 | | | |
| 1966 | 0.00% | 1,473 | | | | | | |
| 1967 | 0.00% | 1,029 | | | | | | |
| 1968* | 0.00% | 2,105 | | | | | | |
| 1969* | 0.00% | 1,975 | | | | | | |
| 1970* | 0.00% | 84 | | | | | | |
| 1971 | 0.00% | 2,095 | | | | | | |
| 1972 | 0.00% | 2,202 | | | | | | |
| 1973 | 0.00% | 3,394 | | | | | | |
| 1974 | 0.00% | (928) | | | | | | |
| 1975 | 0.00% | 1,773 | | | | | | |
| 1976 | 0.00% | 2,528 | | | | | | |
| 1977 | 0.00% | 4,456 | | | | | | |
| 1978 | 0.00% | 3,564 | | | | | | |
| 1979 | 0.00% | 1,931 | | | | | | |
| 1980 | 0.00% | 76 | | | | | | |
| 1981* | 0.00% | (263) | | | | | | |
| 1982 | -20.00% | (531) | (531) | 4,040 | 3,101 | | | |

(1) See Appendix B-4
(2) See Appendix C-1.1
*Does not reflect imposition or removal of surcharge or credit

## Changes in Maximum Income Tax Rates 1983-2011
### Comparison to Employment Increases and Decreases
### Sorted by Year

| Year | Change in Maximum Tax Rate (1) | Employment Increase (2) (Decrease) (thousands) | Employment Increase (Decrease) | | | | | |
|---|---|---|---|---|---|---|---|---|
| | | | Reduction in Tax Rate | | | Increase in Tax Rate | | |
| | | | Year of Change | Years Later | | Year of Change | Years Later | |
| | | | | 1 | 2 | | 1 | 2 |
| 1983 | 0.00% | 4,040 | | | | | | |
| 1984 | 0.00% | 3,101 | | | | | | |
| 1985 | 0.00% | 2,585 | | | | | | |
| 1986 | 0.00% | 2,066 | | | | | | |
| 1987 | -11.50% | 3,063 | 3,063 | 2,692 | 2,373 | | | |
| 1988* | -10.50% | 2,692 | 2,692 | 2,373 | (1,141) | | | |
| 1989* | 0.00% | 2,373 | | | | | | |
| 1990* | 0.00% | (1,141) | | | | | | |
| 1991 | 3.00% | 38 | | | | 38 | 1,097 | 2,891 |
| 1992 | 0.00% | 1,097 | | | | | | |
| 1993 | 8.60% | 2,891 | | | | 2,891 | 2,697 | 462 |
| 1994 | 0.00% | 2,697 | | | | | | |
| 1995 | 0.00% | 462 | | | | | | |
| 1996 | 0.00% | 3,173 | | | | | | |
| 1997 | 0.00% | 2,428 | | | | | | |
| 1998 | 0.00% | 2,301 | | | | | | |
| 1999 | 0.00% | 3,532 | | | | | | |
| 2000 | 0.00% | 1,219 | | | | | | |
| 2001 | -0.50% | (2,077) | (2,077) | 1,716 | 1,055 | | | |
| 2002 | -0.50% | 1,716 | 1,716 | 1,055 | 1,773 | | | |
| 2003 | -3.60% | 1,055 | 1,055 | 1,773 | 2,905 | | | |
| 2004 | 0.00% | 1,773 | | | | | | |
| 2005 | 0.00% | 2,905 | | | | | | |
| 2006 | 0.00% | 2,878 | | | | | | |
| 2007 | 0.00% | 369 | | | | | | |
| 2008 | 0.00% | (4,210) | | | | | | |
| 2009 | 0.00% | (3,687) | | | | | | |
| 2010 | 0.00% | 830 | | | | | | |
| 2011 | 0.00% | 2,307 | | | | | | |

(1) see Appendix B-4

(2) See Appendix C-1.1

*Does not reflect imposition or removal of surcharge or credit

### Changes in Maximum Income Tax Rates 1953-2011
### Comparison to Employment Increases and Decreases
### Sorted by Change in Maximum Tax rate

| Year | Change in Maximum Income Tax Rate (1) | Employment Increase (2) (Decrease) (thousands) | Employment Increase (Decrease) | | | | | |
|---|---|---|---|---|---|---|---|---|
| | | | Reduction in Tax Rate | | | Increase in Tax Rate | | |
| | | | Year of Change | Years Later | | Year of Change | Years Later | |
| | | | | 1 | 2 | | 1 | 2 |
| 1982 | -20.00% | (531) | (531) | 4,040 | 3,101 | | | |
| 1964 | -14.00% | 1,670 | 1,670 | 2,201 | 1,473 | | | |
| 1987 | -11.50% | 3,063 | 3,063 | 2,692 | 2,373 | | | |
| 1988* | -10.50% | 2,692 | 2,692 | 2,373 | (1,141) | | | |
| 1965 | -7.00% | 2,201 | 2,201 | 1,473 | 1,029 | | | |
| 2003 | -3.60% | 1,055 | 1,055 | 1,773 | 2,905 | | | |
| 1954 | -1.00% | 729 | 729 | 3,000 | (121) | | | |
| 2001 | -0.50% | (2,077) | (2,077) | 1,716 | 1,055 | | | |
| 2002 | -0.50% | 1,716 | 1,716 | 1,055 | 1,773 | | | |
| 1991 | 3.00% | 38 | | | | 38 | 1,097 | 2,891 |
| 1993 | 8.60% | 2,891 | | | | 2,891 | 2,697 | 462 |

(1) see Appendix B-4

(2) See Appendix C-1.1

*Does not reflect imposition or removal of surcharge or credit

Appendix A 3.4

## No Change in Maximum Income Tax Rates
### Comparison to Employment Total and Net Increases and Decreases
### 1953-2011
### By Amount of Change in Employment

| Year | Employment Increase (Decrease) (thousands) (1) | Employment Increase | Employment Decrease |
|---|---|---|---|
| 1977 | 4,456 | 4,456 | |
| 1983 | 4,040 | 4,040 | |
| 2 | 8,496 | 4,248 | |
| 1978 | 3,564 | 3,564 | |
| 1999 | 3,532 | 3,532 | |
| 1973 | 3,394 | 3,394 | |
| 1996 | 3,173 | 3,173 | |
| 1984 | 3,101 | 3,101 | |
| 1955 | 3,000 | 3,000 | |
| 6 | 19,764 | 3,294 | |
| 2005 | 2,905 | 2,905 | |
| 2006 | 2,878 | 2,878 | |
| 1994 | 2,697 | 2,697 | |
| 1985 | 2,585 | 2,585 | |
| 1976 | 2,528 | 2,528 | |
| 1997 | 2,428 | 2,428 | |
| 1989* | 2,373 | 2,373 | |
| 2011 | 2,307 | 2,307 | |
| 1998 | 2,301 | 2,301 | |
| 1972 | 2,202 | 2,202 | |
| 1968* | 2,105 | 2,105 | |
| 1971 | 2,095 | 2,095 | |
| 1986 | 2,066 | 2,066 | |
| 13 | 31,470 | 2,421 | |

| Year | Employment Increase (Decrease) (thousands) (1) | Employment Increase | Employment Decrease |
|---|---|---|---|
| 1969* | 1,975 | 1,975 | |
| 1979 | 1,931 | 1,931 | |
| 1975 | 1,773 | 1,773 | |
| 2004 | 1,773 | 1,773 | |
| 1959 | 1,479 | 1,479 | |
| 1966 | 1,473 | 1,473 | |
| 1963 | 1,255 | 1,255 | |
| 2000 | 1,219 | 1,219 | |
| 1992 | 1,097 | 1,097 | |
| 1967 | 1,029 | 1,029 | |
| 10 | 15,004 | 1,500 | |
| 1962 | 964 | 964 | |
| 2010 | 830 | 830 | |
| 1958 | 648 | 648 | |
| 1995 | 462 | 462 | |
| 1960 | 429 | 429 | |
| 2007 | 369 | 369 | |
| 1961 | 332 | 332 | |
| 1970* | 84 | 84 | |
| 1980 | 76 | 76 | |
| 9 | 4,194 | 466 | |
| 1956 | (121) | | (121) |
| 1981* | (263) | | (263) |
| 1,957 | (412) | | (412) |
| 1,974 | (928) | | (928) |
| 1990* | (1,141) | | (1,141) |
| 1,953 | (1,576) | | (1,576) |
| 2,009 | (3,687) | | (3,687) |
| 2,008 | (4,210) | | (4,210) |
| 8 | (12,338) | | (1,542) |

See Appendix C-1.1

*Does not reflect imposition or removal of surcharge or credit

## Maximum and Effective Income Tax Rates 1953-1982
### Comparison to Employment Increases (Decreases)
### By Year

| Year | Employment Increase (1) (Decrease) (thousands) | Maximum Tax Rate (2) | Effective Income Tax Rates | | | |
|---|---|---|---|---|---|---|
| | | | (3) $1,000,000 | (4) $400,000 | (5) $250,000 | (6) $200,000 |
| 1953 | (1,576) | 92.0% | 89.7% | 86.2% | 82.7% | 80.4% |
| 1954 | 729 | 91.0% | 88.5% | 84.7% | 80.9% | 78.4% |
| 1955 | 3,000 | 91.0% | 86.0% | 78.4% | 71.7% | 67.3% |
| 1956 | (121) | 91.0% | 86.0% | 78.4% | 71.7% | 67.3% |
| 1957 | (412) | 91.0% | 86.0% | 78.4% | 71.7% | 67.3% |
| 1958 | 648 | 91.0% | 86.0% | 78.4% | 71.7% | 67.3% |
| 1959 | 1,479 | 91.0% | 86.0% | 78.4% | 71.7% | 67.3% |
| 1960 | 429 | 91.0% | 86.0% | 78.4% | 71.7% | 67.3% |
| 1961 | 332 | 91.0% | 86.0% | 78.4% | 71.7% | 67.3% |
| 1962 | 964 | 91.0% | 86.0% | 78.4% | 71.7% | 67.3% |
| 1963 | 1,255 | 91.0% | 86.0% | 78.4% | 71.7% | 67.3% |
| 1964 | 1,670 | 77.0% | 73.4% | 67.9% | 62.8% | 59.3% |
| 1965 | 2,201 | 70.0% | 67.1% | 62.7% | 58.4% | 55.5% |
| 1966 | 1,473 | 70.0% | 67.1% | 62.7% | 58.4% | 55.5% |
| 1967 | 1,029 | 70.0% | 67.1% | 62.7% | 58.4% | 55.5% |
| 1968* | 2,105 | 70.0% | 72.1% | 67.5% | 62.8% | 59.7% |
| 1969* | 1,975 | 70.0% | 73.8% | 69.0% | 64.2% | 61.0% |
| 1970* | 84 | 70.0% | 68.8% | 64.3% | 59.9% | 56.9% |
| 1971 | 2,095 | 70.0% | 67.1% | 62.7% | 58.4% | 55.5% |
| 1972 | 2,202 | 70.0% | 67.1% | 62.7% | 58.4% | 55.5% |
| 1973 | 3,394 | 70.0% | 67.1% | 62.7% | 58.4% | 55.5% |
| 1974 | (928) | 70.0% | 67.1% | 62.7% | 58.4% | 55.5% |
| 1975 | 1,773 | 70.0% | 67.1% | 62.7% | 58.4% | 55.5% |
| 1976 | 2,528 | 70.0% | 67.1% | 62.7% | 58.4% | 55.5% |
| 1977 | 4,456 | 70.0% | 66.9% | 62.2% | 57.7% | 54.4% |
| 1978 | 3,564 | 70.0% | 66.9% | 62.2% | 57.7% | 54.4% |
| 1979 | 1,931 | 70.0% | 66.7% | 61.7% | 56.7% | 53.5% |
| 1980 | 76 | 70.0% | 66.7% | 61.7% | 56.7% | 53.5% |
| 1981* | (263) | 70.0% | 65.8% | 60.9% | 56.0% | 52.8% |
| 1982 | (531) | 50.0% | 48.7% | 46.9% | 45.0% | 43.7% |

See Appendix A-4.5 for notes and source information

## Maximum and Effective Income Tax Rates 1983-2011
### Comparison to Employment Increases (Decreases)
### By Year

| Year | Employment Increase (Decrease) (thousands) (2) | Maximum Tax Rate (2) | Effective Income Tax Rates | | | |
|------|------|------|------|------|------|------|
| | | | (3) $1,000,000 | (4) $400,000 | (5) $250,000 | (6) $200,000 |
| 1983 | 4,040 | 50.0% | 48.4% | 46.0% | 43.6% | 42.0% |
| 1984 | 3,101 | 50.0% | 48.1% | 45.4% | 42.6% | 40.7% |
| 1985 | 2,585 | 50.0% | 48.1% | 45.2% | 42.3% | 40.3% |
| 1986 | 2,066 | 50.0% | 48.0% | 45.0% | 42.0% | 40.0% |
| 1987 | 3,063 | 38.5% | 37.5% | 36.0% | 34.5% | 33.5% |
| 1988* | 2,692 | 28.0% | 28.1% | 28.3% | 28.5% | 28.5% |
| 1989* | 2,373 | 28.0% | 28.1% | 28.3% | 28.5% | 28.6% |
| 1990* | (1,141) | 28.0% | 28.1% | 28.3% | 28.5% | 28.6% |
| 1991 | 38 | 31.0% | 30.3% | 29.3% | 28.2% | 27.6% |
| 1992 | 1,097 | 31.0% | 30.3% | 29.2% | 28.1% | 27.4% |
| 1993 | 2,891 | 39.6% | 37.3% | 33.7% | 30.2% | 28.8% |
| 1994 | 2,697 | 39.6% | 37.2% | 33.7% | 30.1% | 28.7% |
| 1995 | 462 | 39.6% | 37.2% | 33.5% | 30.0% | 28.5% |
| 1996 | 3,173 | 39.6% | 37.1% | 33.4% | 29.8% | 28.2% |
| 1997 | 2,428 | 39.6% | 37.0% | 33.2% | 29.6% | 28.0% |
| 1998 | 2,301 | 39.6% | 37.0% | 33.0% | 29.5% | 27.8% |
| 1999 | 3,532 | 39.6% | 36.9% | 32.9% | 29.3% | 27.7% |
| 2000 | 1,219 | 39.6% | 36.9% | 32.8% | 29.2% | 27.5% |
| 2001 | (2,077) | 39.1% | 36.3% | 32.1% | 28.6% | 26.9% |
| 2002 | 1,716 | 38.6% | 35.7% | 31.3% | 27.7% | 25.9% |
| 2003 | 1,055 | 35.0% | 32.5% | 28.8% | 25.6% | 23.7% |
| 2004 | 1,773 | 35.0% | 32.5% | 28.7% | 25.4% | 23.5% |
| 2005 | 2,905 | 35.0% | 32.4% | 28.5% | 25.2% | 23.3% |
| 2006 | 2,878 | 35.0% | 32.3% | 28.3% | 25.0% | 23.0% |
| 2007 | 369 | 35.0% | 32.2% | 28.1% | 24.7% | 22.6% |
| 2008 | (4,210) | 35.0% | 32.2% | 27.9% | 24.5% | 22.4% |
| 2009 | (3,687) | 35.0% | 32.0% | 27.6% | 24.1% | 22.1% |
| 2010 | 830 | 35.0% | 32.0% | 27.6% | 24.1% | 22.1% |
| 2011 | 2,307 | 35.0% | 32.0% | 27.5% | 24.0% | 22.0% |

See Appendix A-4.5 for notes and source information

### Maximum and Effective Income Tax Rates 1953-2011
### Comparison to Employment Increases (Decreases)
### By Maximum Income Tax Rate

| Year | Employment Increase (Decrease) (thousands) (1) | Maximum Tax Rate (2) | Effective Income Tax Rates | | | |
|---|---|---|---|---|---|---|
| | | | (3) $1,000,000 | (4) $400,000 | (5) $250,000 | (6) $200,000 |
| 1988* | 2,692 | 28.0% | 28.1% | 28.3% | 28.5% | 28.5% |
| 1989* | 2,373 | 28.0% | 28.1% | 28.3% | 28.5% | 28.6% |
| 1990* | (1,141) | 28.0% | 28.1% | 28.3% | 28.5% | 28.6% |
| 1991 | 38 | 31.0% | 30.3% | 29.3% | 28.2% | 27.6% |
| 1992 | 1,097 | 31.0% | 30.3% | 29.2% | 28.1% | 27.4% |
| 5 | 1,012 | 29.2% | 29.0% | 28.7% | 28.4% | 28.1% |
| 2003 | 1,055 | 35.0% | 32.5% | 28.8% | 25.6% | 23.7% |
| 2004 | 1,773 | 35.0% | 32.5% | 28.7% | 25.4% | 23.5% |
| 2005 | 2,905 | 35.0% | 32.4% | 28.5% | 25.2% | 23.3% |
| 2006 | 2,878 | 35.0% | 32.3% | 28.3% | 25.0% | 23.0% |
| 2007 | 369 | 35.0% | 32.2% | 28.1% | 24.7% | 22.6% |
| 2008 | (4,210) | 35.0% | 32.2% | 27.9% | 24.5% | 22.4% |
| 2009 | (3,687) | 35.0% | 32.0% | 27.6% | 24.1% | 22.1% |
| 2010 | 830 | 35.0% | 32.0% | 27.6% | 24.1% | 22.1% |
| 2011 | 2,307 | 35.0% | 32.0% | 27.5% | 24.0% | 22.0% |
| 9 | 469 | 35.0% | 32.2% | 28.1% | 24.7% | 22.8% |
| 1987 | 3,063 | 38.5% | 37.5% | 36.0% | 34.5% | 33.5% |
| 2002 | 1,716 | 38.6% | 35.7% | 31.3% | 27.7% | 25.9% |
| 2001 | (2,077) | 39.1% | 36.3% | 32.1% | 28.6% | 26.9% |
| 1993 | 2,891 | 39.6% | 37.3% | 33.7% | 30.2% | 28.8% |
| 1994 | 2,697 | 39.6% | 37.2% | 33.7% | 30.1% | 28.7% |
| 1995 | 462 | 39.6% | 37.2% | 33.5% | 30.0% | 28.5% |
| 1996 | 3,173 | 39.6% | 37.1% | 33.4% | 29.8% | 28.2% |
| 1997 | 2,428 | 39.6% | 37.0% | 33.2% | 29.6% | 28.0% |
| 1998 | 2,301 | 39.6% | 37.0% | 33.0% | 29.5% | 27.8% |
| 1999 | 3,532 | 39.6% | 36.9% | 32.9% | 29.3% | 27.7% |
| 2000 | 1,219 | 39.6% | 36.9% | 32.8% | 29.2% | 27.5% |
| 11 | 1,946 | 39.4% | 36.9% | 33.2% | 29.9% | 28.3% |
| 1982 | (531) | 50.0% | 48.7% | 46.9% | 45.0% | 43.7% |
| 1983 | 4,040 | 50.0% | 48.4% | 46.0% | 43.6% | 42.0% |
| 1984 | 3,101 | 50.0% | 48.1% | 45.4% | 42.6% | 40.7% |
| 1985 | 2,585 | 50.0% | 48.1% | 45.2% | 42.3% | 40.3% |
| 1986 | 2,066 | 50.0% | 48.0% | 45.0% | 42.0% | 40.0% |
| 5 | 2,252 | 50.0% | 48.3% | 45.7% | 43.1% | 41.3% |

See Appendix A-4.5 for notes and source information

## Maximum and Effective Income Tax Rates 1953-2011
### Comparison to Employment Increases (Decreases)
### By Maximum Income Tax Rate

| Year | Employment Increase (Decrease) (thousands) (1) | Maximum Tax Rate (2) | Effective Income Tax Rates | | | |
|---|---|---|---|---|---|---|
| | | | (3) $1,000,000 | (4) $400,000 | (5) $250,000 | (6) $200,000 |
| 1965 | 2,201 | 70.0% | 67.1% | 62.7% | 58.4% | 55.5% |
| 1966 | 1,473 | 70.0% | 67.1% | 62.7% | 58.4% | 55.5% |
| 1967 | 1,029 | 70.0% | 67.1% | 62.7% | 58.4% | 55.5% |
| 1968* | 2,105 | 70.0% | 72.1% | 67.5% | 62.8% | 59.7% |
| 1969* | 1,975 | 70.0% | 73.8% | 69.0% | 64.2% | 61.0% |
| 1970* | 84 | 70.0% | 68.8% | 64.3% | 59.9% | 56.9% |
| 1971 | 2,095 | 70.0% | 67.1% | 62.7% | 58.4% | 55.5% |
| 1972 | 2,202 | 70.0% | 67.1% | 62.7% | 58.4% | 55.5% |
| 1973 | 3,394 | 70.0% | 67.1% | 62.7% | 58.4% | 55.5% |
| 1974 | (928) | 70.0% | 67.1% | 62.7% | 58.4% | 55.5% |
| 1975 | 1,773 | 70.0% | 67.1% | 62.7% | 58.4% | 55.5% |
| 1976 | 2,528 | 70.0% | 67.1% | 62.7% | 58.4% | 55.5% |
| 1977 | 4,456 | 70.0% | 66.9% | 62.2% | 57.7% | 54.4% |
| 1978 | 3,564 | 70.0% | 66.9% | 62.2% | 57.7% | 54.4% |
| 1979 | 1,931 | 70.0% | 66.7% | 61.7% | 56.7% | 53.5% |
| 1980 | 76 | 70.0% | 66.7% | 61.7% | 56.7% | 53.5% |
| 1981* | (263) | 70.0% | 65.8% | 60.9% | 56.0% | 52.8% |
| 1964 | 1,670 | 77.0% | 73.4% | 67.9% | 62.8% | 59.3% |
| 18 | 1,743 | 70.4% | 68.0% | 63.4% | 58.9% | 55.8% |
| 1954 | 729 | 91.0% | 88.5% | 84.7% | 80.9% | 78.4% |
| 1955 | 3,000 | 91.0% | 86.0% | 78.4% | 71.7% | 67.3% |
| 1956 | (121) | 91.0% | 86.0% | 78.4% | 71.7% | 67.3% |
| 1957 | (412) | 91.0% | 86.0% | 78.4% | 71.7% | 67.3% |
| 1958 | 648 | 91.0% | 86.0% | 78.4% | 71.7% | 67.3% |
| 1959 | 1,479 | 91.0% | 86.0% | 78.4% | 71.7% | 67.3% |
| 1960 | 429 | 91.0% | 86.0% | 78.4% | 71.7% | 67.3% |
| 1961 | 332 | 91.0% | 86.0% | 78.4% | 71.7% | 67.3% |
| 1962 | 964 | 91.0% | 86.0% | 78.4% | 71.7% | 67.3% |
| 1963 | 1,255 | 91.0% | 86.0% | 78.4% | 71.7% | 67.3% |
| 1953 | (1,576) | 92.0% | 89.7% | 86.2% | 82.7% | 80.4% |
| 11 | 612 | 91.1% | 86.5% | 79.7% | 73.5% | 69.5% |

See Appendix A-4.5 for notes and source information

Notes To Appendices A 4.1 to A 4.4
Maximum and Effective Income Tax Rates 1983-2011
Comparison to Employment Increases (Decreases)

(1) See Appendix C 1.1
(2) See Appendix B 1.1
(3) See Appendix B 3.1
(4) See Appendix B 4.1
(5) See Appendix B 5.1
(6) See Appendix B 6.1
(7) See Appendix B 3.2
(8) See Appendix B 4.2
(9) See Appendix B 5.2
(10) See Appendix B 6.2
(11) See Appendices A 4.1 and A 4.2
* See Appendices B 3.3, B 4.3, B 5.3 and B 6.3 for impact of surcharges and credit

## Maximum and Effective Income Tax Rates - $1,000,000 Taxable Income
### Comparison to Employment Increases (Decreases)
### 1953-1982

| Year | Maximum Tax Rate (1) | Effective Tax Rate $1,000,000 Taxable Income (2) | Employment Increase (Decrease) (thousands) (3) | Employment | |
|---|---|---|---|---|---|
| | | | | Increase (thousands) | Decrease (thousands) |
| 1953 | 92.0% | 89.7% | (1,576) | | (1,576) |
| 1954 | 91.0% | 88.5% | 729 | 729 | |
| 1955 | 91.0% | 86.0% | 3,000 | 3,000 | |
| 1956 | 91.0% | 86.0% | (121) | | (121) |
| 1957 | 91.0% | 86.0% | (412) | | (412) |
| 1958 | 91.0% | 86.0% | 648 | 648 | |
| 1959 | 91.0% | 86.0% | 1,479 | 1,479 | |
| 1960 | 91.0% | 86.0% | 429 | 429 | |
| 1961 | 91.0% | 86.0% | 332 | 332 | |
| 1962 | 91.0% | 86.0% | 964 | 964 | |
| 1963 | 91.0% | 86.0% | 1,255 | 1,255 | |
| 1964 | 77.0% | 73.4% | 1,670 | 1,670 | |
| 1965 | 70.0% | 67.1% | 2,201 | 2,201 | |
| 1966 | 70.0% | 67.1% | 1,473 | 1,473 | |
| 1967 | 70.0% | 67.1% | 1,029 | 1,029 | |
| 1968* | 70.0% | 72.1% | 2,105 | 2,105 | |
| 1969* | 70.0% | 73.8% | 1,975 | 1,975 | |
| 1970* | 70.0% | 68.8% | 84 | 84 | |
| 1971 | 70.0% | 67.1% | 2,095 | 2,095 | |
| 1972 | 70.0% | 67.1% | 2,202 | 2,202 | |
| 1973 | 70.0% | 67.1% | 3,394 | 3,394 | |
| 1974 | 70.0% | 67.1% | (928) | | (928) |
| 1975 | 70.0% | 67.1% | 1,773 | 1,773 | |
| 1976 | 70.0% | 67.1% | 2,528 | 2,528 | |
| 1977 | 70.0% | 66.9% | 4,456 | 4,456 | |
| 1978 | 70.0% | 66.9% | 3,564 | 3,564 | |
| 1979 | 70.0% | 66.7% | 1,931 | 1,931 | |
| 1980 | 70.0% | 66.7% | 76 | 76 | |
| 1981* | 70.0% | 65.8% | (263) | | (263) |
| 1982 | 50.0% | 48.7% | (531) | | (531) |

(1) See Appendix B 1.1          (2) See Appendix B 3.1
(3) See Appendix C 1.1
* See Appendix B 3.3 for impact of surcharges and credit

Maximum and Effective Income Tax Rates - $1,000,000 Taxable Income
Comparison to Employment Increases (Decreases)
1983-2011

| Year | Maximum Tax Rate (1) | Effective Tax Rate $1,000,000 Taxable Income (2) | Employment Increase (Decrease) (thousands) (3) | Employment | |
|---|---|---|---|---|---|
| | | | | Increase (thousands) | Decrease (thousands) |
| 1983 | 50.0% | 48.4% | 4,040 | 4,040 | |
| 1984 | 50.0% | 48.1% | 3,101 | 3,101 | |
| 1985 | 50.0% | 48.1% | 2,585 | 2,585 | |
| 1986 | 50.0% | 48.0% | 2,066 | 2,066 | |
| 1987 | 38.5% | 37.5% | 3,063 | 3,063 | |
| 1988* | 28.0% | 28.1% | 2,692 | 2,692 | |
| 1989* | 28.0% | 28.1% | 2,373 | 38 | |
| 1990* | 28.0% | 28.1% | (1,141) | | (1,141) |
| 1991 | 31.0% | 30.3% | 38 | 38 | |
| 1992 | 31.0% | 30.3% | 1,097 | 1,097 | |
| 1993 | 39.6% | 37.3% | 2,891 | 2,891 | |
| 1994 | 39.6% | 37.2% | 2,697 | 2,697 | |
| 1995 | 39.6% | 37.2% | 462 | 462 | |
| 1996 | 39.6% | 37.1% | 3,173 | 3,173 | |
| 1997 | 39.6% | 37.0% | 2,428 | 2,428 | |
| 1998 | 39.6% | 37.0% | 2,301 | 2,301 | |
| 1999 | 39.6% | 36.9% | 3,532 | 3,532 | |
| 2000 | 39.6% | 36.9% | 1,219 | 1,219 | |
| 2001 | 39.1% | 36.3% | (2,077) | | (2,077) |
| 2002 | 38.6% | 35.7% | 1,716 | 1,716 | |
| 2003 | 35.0% | 32.5% | 1,055 | 1,055 | |
| 2004 | 35.0% | 32.5% | 1,773 | 1,773 | |
| 2005 | 35.0% | 32.4% | 2,905 | 2,905 | |
| 2006 | 35.0% | 32.3% | 2,878 | 2,878 | |
| 2007 | 35.0% | 32.2% | 369 | 369 | |
| 2008 | 35.0% | 32.2% | (4,210) | | (4,210) |
| 2009 | 35.0% | 32.0% | (3,687) | | (3,687) |
| 2010 | 35.0% | 32.0% | 830 | 830 | |
| 2011 | 35.0% | 32.0% | 2,307 | 2,307 | |

(1) See Appendix B 1.1        (2) See Appendix B 3.1
(3) See Appendix C 1.1
* See Appendix B 3.3 for impact of surcharges and credit

## Maximum and Effective Income Tax Rates - $1,000,000 Taxable Income
### Comparison to Employment Increases (Decreases)
### 1953-2011

| Year | Maximum Tax Rate (1) | Effective Tax Rate $1,000,000 Taxable Income (2) | Employment Increase (Decrease) (thousands) (3) | Employment Increase (thousands) | Employment Decrease (thousands) |
|---|---|---|---|---|---|
| 1988* | 28.0% | 28.1% | 2,692 | 2,692 | |
| 1989* | 28.0% | 28.1% | 2,373 | 2,373 | |
| 1990* | 28.0% | 28.1% | (1,141) | | (1,141) |
| 1992 | 31.0% | 30.3% | 1,097 | 1,097 | |
| 1991 | 31.0% | 30.3% | 38 | 38 | |
| 5 | 29.2% | 29.0% | 1,012 | 6,200 | (1,141) |
| 2011 | 35.0% | 32.0% | 2,307 | 2,307 | |
| 2010 | 35.0% | 32.0% | 830 | 830 | |
| 2009 | 35.0% | 32.0% | (3,687) | | (3,687) |
| 2008 | 35.0% | 32.2% | (4,210) | | (4,210) |
| 2007 | 35.0% | 32.2% | 369 | 369 | |
| 2006 | 35.0% | 32.3% | 2,878 | 2,878 | |
| 2005 | 35.0% | 32.4% | 2,905 | 2,905 | |
| 2004 | 35.0% | 32.5% | 1,773 | 1,773 | |
| 2003 | 35.0% | 32.5% | 1,055 | 1,055 | |
| 9 | 35.0% | 32.2% | 469 | 12,117 | (7,897) |
| 2002 | 38.6% | 35.7% | 1,716 | 1,716 | |
| 2001 | 39.1% | 36.3% | (2,077) | | (2,077) |
| 2000 | 39.6% | 36.9% | 1,219 | 1,219 | |
| 1999 | 39.6% | 36.9% | 3,532 | 3,532 | |
| 1998 | 39.6% | 37.0% | 2,301 | 2,301 | |
| 1997 | 39.6% | 37.0% | 2,428 | 2,428 | |
| 1996 | 39.6% | 37.1% | 3,173 | 3,173 | |
| 1995 | 39.6% | 37.2% | 462 | 462 | |
| 1994 | 39.6% | 37.2% | 2,697 | 2,697 | |
| 1993 | 39.6% | 37.3% | 2,891 | 2,891 | |
| 1987 | 38.5% | 37.5% | 3,063 | 3,063 | |
| 11 | 39.4% | 36.9% | 1,946 | 23,482 | (2,077) |
| 1986 | 50.0% | 48.0% | 2,066 | 2,066 | |
| 1985 | 50.0% | 48.1% | 2,585 | 2,585 | |
| 1984 | 50.0% | 48.1% | 3,101 | 3,101 | |
| 1983 | 50.0% | 48.4% | 4,040 | 4,040 | |
| 1982 | 50.0% | 48.7% | (531) | | (531) |
| 5 | 50.0% | 48.3% | 2,252 | 11,792 | (531) |

(1) See Appendix B 1.1
(2) See Appendices A 5.1 and A 5.2
(3) See Appendix C 1.1
* See Appendix B 3.3 for impact of surcharges and credit

## Maximum and Effective Income Tax Rates - $1,000,000 Taxable Income
### Comparison to Employment Increases (Decreases)
### 1953-2011

| Year | Maximum Tax Rate (1) | Effective Tax Rate $1,000,000 Taxable Income (2) | Employment Increase (Decrease) (thousands) (3) | Employment | |
|---|---|---|---|---|---|
| | | | | Increase (thousands) | Decrease (thousands) |
| 1981* | 70.0% | 65.8% | (263) | | (263) |
| 1979 | 70.0% | 66.7% | 1,931 | 1,931 | |
| 1980 | 70.0% | 66.7% | 76 | 76 | |
| 1977 | 70.0% | 66.9% | 4,456 | 4,456 | |
| 1978 | 70.0% | 66.9% | 3,564 | 3,564 | |
| 1965 | 70.0% | 67.1% | 2,201 | 2,201 | |
| 1966 | 70.0% | 67.1% | 1,473 | 1,473 | |
| 1967 | 70.0% | 67.1% | 1,029 | 1,029 | |
| 1971 | 70.0% | 67.1% | 2,095 | 2,095 | |
| 1972 | 70.0% | 67.1% | 2,202 | 2,202 | |
| 1973 | 70.0% | 67.1% | 3,394 | 3,394 | |
| 1974 | 70.0% | 67.1% | (928) | | (928) |
| 1975 | 70.0% | 67.1% | 1,773 | 1,773 | |
| 1976 | 70.0% | 67.1% | 2,528 | 2,528 | |
| 1970* | 70.0% | 68.8% | 84 | 84 | |
| 1968* | 70.0% | 72.1% | 2,105 | 2,105 | |
| 1964 | 77.0% | 73.4% | 1,670 | 1,670 | |
| 1969* | 70.0% | 73.8% | 1,975 | 1,975 | |
| 18 | 70.4% | 68.0% | 1,743 | 32,556 | (1,191) |
| 1955 | 91.0% | 86.0% | 3,000 | 3,000 | |
| 1956 | 91.0% | 86.0% | (121) | | (121) |
| 1957 | 91.0% | 86.0% | (412) | | (412) |
| 1958 | 91.0% | 86.0% | 648 | 648 | |
| 1959 | 91.0% | 86.0% | 1,479 | 1,479 | |
| 1960 | 91.0% | 86.0% | 429 | 429 | |
| 1961 | 91.0% | 86.0% | 332 | 332 | |
| 1962 | 91.0% | 86.0% | 964 | 964 | |
| 1963 | 91.0% | 86.0% | 1,255 | 1,255 | |
| 1954 | 91.0% | 88.5% | 729 | 729 | |
| 1953 | 92.0% | 89.7% | (1,576) | | (1,576) |
| 11 | 91.1% | 86.5% | 612 | 8,836 | (2,109) |

(1) See Appendix B 1.1
(2) See Appendices A 5.1 and A 5.2
(3) See Appendix C 1.1
* See Appendix B 3.3 for impact of surcharges and credit

## Changes in Effective Income Tax Rates 1953-1982
## Comparison to Employment Increases and Decreases
### Sorted by Year

| Year | Maximum Tax Rate (1) | Effective Tax Rate $1,000,000 Taxable Income (2) | Change in Effective Tax Rate (3) | Employment Increase (4) (Decrease) (thousands) |
|---|---|---|---|---|
| 1953 | 92.0% | 89.7% | 0.0% | (1,576) |
| 1954 | 91.0% | 88.5% | -1.2% | 729 |
| 1955 | 91.0% | 86.0% | -2.5% | 3,000 |
| 1956 | 91.0% | 86.0% | 0.0% | (121) |
| 1957 | 91.0% | 86.0% | 0.0% | (412) |
| 1958 | 91.0% | 86.0% | 0.0% | 648 |
| 1959 | 91.0% | 86.0% | 0.0% | 1,479 |
| 1960 | 91.0% | 86.0% | 0.0% | 429 |
| 1961 | 91.0% | 86.0% | 0.0% | 332 |
| 1962 | 91.0% | 86.0% | 0.0% | 964 |
| 1963 | 91.0% | 86.0% | 0.0% | 1,255 |
| 1964 | 77.0% | 73.4% | -12.6% | 1,670 |
| 1965 | 70.0% | 67.1% | -6.3% | 2,201 |
| 1966 | 70.0% | 67.1% | 0.0% | 1,473 |
| 1967 | 70.0% | 67.1% | 0.0% | 1,029 |
| 1968* | 70.0% | 72.1% | 5.0% | 2,105 |
| 1969* | 70.0% | 73.8% | 1.7% | 1,975 |
| 1970* | 70.0% | 68.8% | -5.0% | 84 |
| 1971 | 70.0% | 67.1% | -1.7% | 2,095 |
| 1972 | 70.0% | 67.1% | 0.0% | 2,202 |
| 1973 | 70.0% | 67.1% | 0.0% | 3,394 |
| 1974 | 70.0% | 67.1% | 0.0% | (928) |
| 1975 | 70.0% | 67.1% | 0.0% | 1,773 |
| 1976 | 70.0% | 67.1% | 0.0% | 2,528 |
| 1977 | 70.0% | 66.9% | -0.2% | 4,456 |
| 1978 | 70.0% | 66.9% | 0.0% | 3,564 |
| 1979 | 70.0% | 66.7% | -0.2% | 1,931 |
| 1980 | 70.0% | 66.7% | 0.0% | 76 |
| 1981* | 70.0% | 65.8% | -0.8% | (263) |
| 1982 | 50.0% | 48.7% | -17.1% | (531) |

(1) See Appendix B 1.1

(2) See Appendix B 3.1

(3) Effective tax rate in each year - Effective tax rate the preceding year

(4) See Appendix C 1.1

* See Appendix B 3.3 for impact of surcharges and credit

### Changes in Effective Income Tax Rates 1983-2011
### Comparison to Employment Increases and Decreases
### Sorted by Year

| Year | Maximum Tax Rate (1) | Effective Tax Rate $1,000,000 Taxable Income (2) | Change in Effective Tax Rate (3) | Employment Increase (4) (Decrease) (thousands) |
|------|------|------|------|------|
| 1983 | 50.0% | 48.4% | -0.3% | 4,040 |
| 1984 | 50.0% | 48.1% | -0.3% | 3,101 |
| 1985 | 50.0% | 48.1% | -0.1% | 2,585 |
| 1986 | 50.0% | 48.0% | -0.1% | 2,066 |
| 1987 | 38.5% | 37.5% | -10.5% | 3,063 |
| 1988* | 28.0% | 28.1% | -9.4% | 2,692 |
| 1989* | 28.0% | 28.1% | 0.0% | 2,373 |
| 1990* | 28.0% | 28.1% | 0.0% | (1,141) |
| 1991 | 31.0% | 30.3% | 2.2% | 38 |
| 1992 | 31.0% | 30.3% | 0.0% | 1,097 |
| 1993 | 39.6% | 37.3% | 7.0% | 2,891 |
| 1994 | 39.6% | 37.2% | 0.0% | 2,697 |
| 1995 | 39.6% | 37.2% | -0.1% | 462 |
| 1996 | 39.6% | 37.1% | -0.1% | 3,173 |
| 1997 | 39.6% | 37.0% | -0.1% | 2,428 |
| 1998 | 39.6% | 37.0% | -0.1% | 2,301 |
| 1999 | 39.6% | 36.9% | 0.0% | 3,532 |
| 2000 | 39.6% | 36.9% | 0.0% | 1,219 |
| 2001 | 39.1% | 36.3% | -0.6% | (2,077) |
| 2002 | 38.6% | 35.7% | -0.6% | 1,716 |
| 2003 | 35.0% | 32.5% | -3.2% | 1,055 |
| 2004 | 35.0% | 32.5% | -0.1% | 1,773 |
| 2005 | 35.0% | 32.4% | -0.1% | 2,905 |
| 2006 | 35.0% | 32.3% | -0.1% | 2,878 |
| 2007 | 35.0% | 32.2% | -0.1% | 369 |
| 2008 | 35.0% | 32.2% | -0.1% | (4,210) |
| 2009 | 35.0% | 32.0% | -0.1% | (3,687) |
| 2010 | 35.0% | 32.0% | 0.0% | 830 |
| 2011 | 35.0% | 32.0% | 0.0% | 2,307 |

(1) See Appendix B 1.1

(2) See Appendix B 3.2

(3) Effective tax rate in each year - Effective tax rate the preceding year

(4) See Appendix C 1.1

* See Appendix B 3.3 for impact of surcharges and credit

Changes in Effective Income Tax Rates 1953-2011
Comparison to Employment Increases and Decreases
Sorted by Year

| Year | Maximum Tax Rate (1) | Effective Tax Rate $1,000,000 Taxable Income (2) | Change in Effective Tax Rate (2) | Employment Increase (3) (Decrease) (thousands) |
|---|---|---|---|---|
| 1982 | 50.0% | 48.7% | -17.094% | (531) |
| 1964 | 77.0% | 73.4% | -12.596% | 1,670 |
| 1987 | 38.5% | 37.5% | -10.499% | 3,063 |
| 1988* | 28.0% | 28.1% | -9.385% | 2,692 |
| 1965 | 70.0% | 67.1% | -6.270% | 2,201 |
| 1970* | 70.0% | 68.8% | -5.032% | 84 |
| 2003 | 35.0% | 32.5% | -3.155% | 1,055 |
| 1955 | 91.0% | 86.0% | -2.518% | 3,000 |
| 1971 | 70.0% | 67.1% | -1.677% | 2,095 |
| 1954 | 91.0% | 88.5% | -1.190% | 729 |
| 1981* | 70.0% | 65.8% | -0.833% | (263) |
| 2002 | 38.6% | 35.7% | -0.628% | 1,716 |
| 2001 | 39.1% | 36.3% | -0.563% | (2,077) |
| 1983 | 50.0% | 48.4% | -0.345% | 4,040 |
| 1984 | 50.0% | 48.1% | -0.260% | 3,101 |
| 1977 | 70.0% | 66.9% | -0.224% | 4,456 |
| 1979 | 70.0% | 66.7% | -0.202% | 1,931 |
| 2009 | 35.0% | 32.0% | -0.121% | (3,687) |
| 2007 | 35.0% | 32.2% | -0.104% | 369 |
| 2006 | 35.0% | 32.3% | -0.081% | 2,878 |
| 1985 | 50.0% | 48.1% | -0.076% | 2,585 |
| 1986 | 50.0% | 48.0% | -0.071% | 2,066 |
| 1998 | 39.6% | 37.0% | -0.071% | 2,301 |
| 1996 | 39.6% | 37.1% | -0.069% | 3,173 |
| 1997 | 39.6% | 37.0% | -0.069% | 2,428 |
| 2008 | 35.0% | 32.2% | -0.063% | (4,210) |
| 1995 | 39.6% | 37.2% | -0.062% | 462 |
| 2005 | 35.0% | 32.4% | -0.058% | 2,905 |
| 2004 | 35.0% | 32.5% | -0.056% | 1,773 |
| 2000 | 39.6% | 36.9% | -0.049% | 1,219 |

(1) See Appendix B 1.1
(2) See Appendices A 6.1 and A 6.2
(3) See Appendix C 1.1
* See Appendix B 3.3 for impact of surcharges and credit

Changes in Effective Income Tax Rates 1953-2011
Comparison to Employment Increases and Decreases
Sorted by Year

| Year | Maximum Tax Rate (1) | Effective Tax Rate $1,000,000 Taxable Income (2) | Change in Effective Tax Rate (2) | Employment Increase (3) (Decrease) (thousands) |
|---|---|---|---|---|
| 1999 | 39.6% | 36.9% | -0.044% | 3,532 |
| 2011 | 35.0% | 32.0% | -0.044% | 2,307 |
| 1992 | 31.0% | 30.3% | -0.036% | 1,097 |
| 1994 | 39.6% | 37.2% | -0.022% | 2,697 |
| 2010 | 35.0% | 32.0% | -0.005% | 830 |
| 1953 | 92.0% | 89.7% | 0.000% | (1,576) |
| 1956 | 91.0% | 86.0% | 0.000% | (121) |
| 1957 | 91.0% | 86.0% | 0.000% | (412) |
| 1958 | 91.0% | 86.0% | 0.000% | 648 |
| 1959 | 91.0% | 86.0% | 0.000% | 1,479 |
| 1960 | 91.0% | 86.0% | 0.000% | 429 |
| 1961 | 91.0% | 86.0% | 0.000% | 332 |
| 1962 | 91.0% | 86.0% | 0.000% | 964 |
| 1963 | 91.0% | 86.0% | 0.000% | 1,255 |
| 1966 | 70.0% | 67.1% | 0.000% | 1,473 |
| 1967 | 70.0% | 67.1% | 0.000% | 1,029 |
| 1972 | 70.0% | 67.1% | 0.000% | 2,202 |
| 1973 | 70.0% | 67.1% | 0.000% | 3,394 |
| 1974 | 70.0% | 67.1% | 0.000% | (928) |
| 1975 | 70.0% | 67.1% | 0.000% | 1,773 |
| 1976 | 70.0% | 67.1% | 0.000% | 2,528 |
| 1978 | 70.0% | 66.9% | 0.000% | 3,564 |
| 1980 | 70.0% | 66.7% | 0.000% | 76 |
| 1990* | 28.0% | 28.1% | 0.003% | (1,141) |
| 1989* | 28.0% | 28.1% | 0.003% | 2,373 |
| 1969* | 70.0% | 73.8% | 1.677% | 1,975 |
| 1991 | 31.0% | 30.3% | 2.197% | 38 |
| 1968* | 70.0% | 72.1% | 5.032% | 2,105 |
| 1993 | 39.6% | 37.3% | 6.978% | 2,891 |

(1) See Appendix B 1.1
(2) See Appendices A 6.1 and A 6.2
(3) See Appendix C 1.1
* See Appendix B 3.3 for impact of surcharges and credit

### Change in Effective Income Tax Rates - $1,0000,000 Taxable Income 1953-2011
### Result of Decreases and Increases in Effective Tax Rate
### Comparison to Employment Increases (Decreases)

| Year | Maximum Tax Rate (1) | Effective Tax Rate $1,000,000 Taxable Income (2) | Change in Effective Tax Rate (2) | Employment (3) (thousands) Increase (Decrease) | Increase | (Decrease) |
|---|---|---|---|---|---|---|
| 1982 | 50.0% | 48.7% | -17.1% | (531) | (531) | |
| 1964 | 77.0% | 73.4% | -12.6% | 1,670 | 1,670 | |
| 1987 | 38.5% | 37.5% | -10.5% | 3,063 | 3,063 | |
| 1988* | 28.0% | 28.1% | -9.4% | 2,692 | 2,692 | |
| 1965 | 70.0% | 67.1% | -6.3% | 2,201 | 2,201 | |
| 1970* | 70.0% | 68.8% | -5.0% | 84 | 84 | |
| 2003 | 35.0% | 32.5% | -3.2% | 1,055 | 1,055 | |
| 1955 | 91.0% | 86.0% | -2.5% | 3,000 | 3,000 | |
| 1971 | 70.0% | 67.1% | -1.7% | 2,095 | 2,095 | |
| 1954 | 91.0% | 88.5% | -1.2% | 729 | 729 | |
| 1981* | 70.0% | 65.8% | -0.8% | (263) | (263) | |
| 2002 | 38.6% | 35.7% | -0.6% | 1,716 | 1,716 | |
| 2001 | 39.1% | 36.3% | -0.6% | (2,077) | (2,077) | |
| 1977 | 70.0% | 66.9% | -0.2% | 4,456 | 4,456 | |
| 1979 | 70.0% | 66.7% | -0.2% | 1,931 | 1,931 | |
| 1969* | 70.0% | 73.8% | 1.7% | 1,975 | | 1,975 |
| 1991 | 31.0% | 30.3% | 2.2% | 38 | | 38 |
| 1968* | 70.0% | 72.1% | 5.0% | 2,105 | | 2,105 |
| 1993 | 39.6% | 37.3% | 7.0% | 2,891 | | 2,891 |
| | | | Total | 28,830 | 21,821 | 7,009 |
| | | | Average | 1,517 | 1,455 | 1,752 |

(1) See Appendix B 1.1

(2) See Appendices A 6.1 and A 6.2

(3) See Appendix C 1.1

* See Appendix B 3.3 for impact of surcharges and credit

## Change in Effective Income Tax Rates - $1,000,000 Taxable Income
### Result of Inflation Adjustments 1953-2011
### Comparison to Employment Increases (Decreases)

| Year | Maximum Tax Rate (1) | Effective Tax Rate $1,000,000 Taxable Income (2) | Change in Effective Tax Rate (2) | Employment (3) (thousands) | | |
|---|---|---|---|---|---|---|
| | | | | Increase (Decrease) | Increase | (Decrease) |
| 1990* | 28.0% | 28.1% | 0.003% | (1,141) | | (1,141) |
| 1989* | 28.0% | 28.1% | 0.003% | 2,373 | 2,373 | |
| 1992 | 31.0% | 30.3% | -0.036% | 1,097 | 1,097 | |
| 2011 | 35.0% | 32.0% | -0.044% | 2,307 | 2,307 | |
| 2010 | 35.0% | 32.0% | -0.005% | 830 | 830 | |
| 2009 | 35.0% | 32.0% | -0.121% | (3,687) | | (3,687) |
| 2008 | 35.0% | 32.2% | -0.063% | (4,210) | | (4,210) |
| 2007 | 35.0% | 32.2% | -0.104% | 369 | 369 | |
| 2006 | 35.0% | 32.3% | -0.081% | 2,878 | 2,878 | |
| 2005 | 35.0% | 32.4% | -0.058% | 2,905 | 2,905 | |
| 2004 | 35.0% | 32.5% | -0.056% | 1,773 | 1,773 | |
| 11 | 33.4% | 31.3% | -0.1% | 5,494 | 14,532 | (9,038) |
| 2000 | 39.6% | 36.9% | -0.049% | 1,219 | 1,219 | |
| 1999 | 39.6% | 36.9% | -0.044% | 3,532 | 3,532 | |
| 1998 | 39.6% | 37.0% | -0.071% | 2,301 | 2,301 | |
| 1997 | 39.6% | 37.0% | -0.069% | 2,428 | 2,428 | |
| 1996 | 39.6% | 37.1% | -0.069% | 3,173 | 3,173 | |
| 1995 | 39.6% | 37.2% | -0.062% | 462 | 462 | |
| 1994 | 39.6% | 37.2% | -0.022% | 2,697 | 2,697 | |
| 7 | 39.6% | 37.0% | -0.1% | 15,812 | 15,812 | 0 |
| 1986 | 50.0% | 48.0% | -0.071% | 2,066 | 2,066 | |
| 1985 | 50.0% | 48.1% | -0.076% | 2,585 | 2,585 | |
| 1984 | 50.0% | 48.1% | -0.260% | 3,101 | 3,101 | |
| 1983 | 50.0% | 48.4% | -0.345% | 4,040 | 4,040 | |
| 4 | 50.0% | 48.1% | -0.2% | 11,792 | 11,792 | 0 |
| | | | Total | 33,098 | 42,136 | (9,038) |
| | | | Average | 1,504 | 2,218 | (3,013) |

(1) See Appendix B 1.1

(2) See Appendices A 6.1 and A 6.2

(3) See Appendix C 1.1

* See Appendix B 3.3 for impact of surcharges and credit

## No Change in Effective Income Tax Rates 1953-2011
## Based on $1,000,000 Taxable Income
## Comparison to Employment Increases (Decreases)

| Year | Maximum Income Tax Rate (1) | Effective Tax Rate $1,000,000 Taxable Income (2) | Employment (3) (thousands) | | |
|---|---|---|---|---|---|
| | | | Increase (Decrease) | Increase | (Decrease) |
| 1980 | 70.0% | 66.7% | 76 | 76 | |
| 1978 | 70.0% | 66.9% | 3,564 | 3,564 | |
| 1966 | 70.0% | 67.1% | 1,473 | 1,473 | |
| 1967 | 70.0% | 67.1% | 1,029 | 1,029 | |
| 1972 | 70.0% | 67.1% | 2,202 | 2,202 | |
| 1973 | 70.0% | 67.1% | 3,394 | 3,394 | |
| 1974 | 70.0% | 67.1% | (928) | | (928) |
| 1975 | 70.0% | 67.1% | 1,773 | 1,773 | |
| 1976 | 70.0% | 67.1% | 2,528 | 2,528 | |
| 9 | 70.0% | 67.0% | 15,111 | 16,039 | (928) |
| 1956 | 91.0% | 86.0% | (121) | | (121) |
| 1957 | 91.0% | 86.0% | (412) | | (412) |
| 1958 | 91.0% | 86.0% | 648 | 648 | |
| 1959 | 91.0% | 86.0% | 1,479 | 1,479 | |
| 1960 | 91.0% | 86.0% | 429 | 429 | |
| 1961 | 91.0% | 86.0% | 332 | 332 | |
| 1962 | 91.0% | 86.0% | 964 | 964 | |
| 1963 | 91.0% | 86.0% | 1,255 | 1,255 | |
| 1953 | 92.0% | 89.7% | (1,576) | | (1,576) |
| 9 | 91.1% | 86.4% | 2,998 | 5,107 | (2,109) |
| | | Total | 18,109 | 21,146 | (3,037) |
| | | Average | 1,006 | 1,175 | (169) |

(1) See Appendix B 1.1

(2) See Appendices A 6.1 and A 6.2

(3) See Appendix C 1.1

* See Appendix B 3.3 for impact of surcharges and credit

## Maximum and Effective Income Tax Rates - $250,000 Taxable Income
### Comparison to Employment Increases (Decreases)
### 1953-1982

| Year | Maximum Tax Rate (1) | Effective Tax Rate $250,000 Taxable Income (2) | Employment (3) (thousands) | | |
|------|------|------|------|------|------|
| | | | Increase (Decrease) | Increase | (Decrease) |
| 1953 | 92.0% | 82.7% | (1,576) | | (1,576) |
| 1954 | 91.0% | 80.9% | 729 | 729 | |
| 1955 | 91.0% | 71.7% | 3,000 | 3,000 | |
| 1956 | 91.0% | 71.7% | (121) | | (121) |
| 1957 | 91.0% | 71.7% | (412) | | (412) |
| 1958 | 91.0% | 71.7% | 648 | 648 | |
| 1959 | 91.0% | 71.7% | 1,479 | 1,479 | |
| 1960 | 91.0% | 71.7% | 429 | 429 | |
| 1961 | 91.0% | 71.7% | 332 | 332 | |
| 1962 | 91.0% | 71.7% | 964 | 964 | |
| 1963 | 91.0% | 71.7% | 1,255 | 1,255 | |
| 1964 | 77.0% | 62.8% | 1,670 | 1,670 | |
| 1965 | 70.0% | 58.4% | 2,201 | 2,201 | |
| 1966 | 70.0% | 58.4% | 1,473 | 1,473 | |
| 1967 | 70.0% | 58.4% | 1,029 | 1,029 | |
| 1968* | 70.0% | 62.8% | 2,105 | 2,105 | |
| 1969* | 70.0% | 64.2% | 1,975 | 1,975 | |
| 1970* | 70.0% | 59.9% | 84 | 84 | |
| 1971 | 70.0% | 58.4% | 2,095 | 2,095 | |
| 1972 | 70.0% | 58.4% | 2,202 | 2,202 | |
| 1973 | 70.0% | 58.4% | 3,394 | 3,394 | |
| 1974 | 70.0% | 58.4% | (928) | | (928) |
| 1975 | 70.0% | 58.4% | 1,773 | 1,773 | |
| 1976 | 70.0% | 58.4% | 2,528 | 2,528 | |
| 1977 | 70.0% | 57.7% | 4,456 | 4,456 | |
| 1978 | 70.0% | 57.7% | 3,564 | 3,564 | |
| 1979 | 70.0% | 56.7% | 1,931 | 1,931 | |
| 1980 | 70.0% | 56.7% | 76 | 76 | |
| 1981* | 70.0% | 56.0% | (263) | | (263) |
| 1982 | 50.0% | 45.0% | (531) | | (531) |

(1) See Appendix B 1.1
(2) See Appendix B 5.1
(3) See Appendix C 1.1
* See Appendix B 5.3 for impact of surcharges and credit

## Maximum and Effective Income Tax Rates - $250,000 Taxable Income
### Comparison to Employment Increases (Decreases)
### 1983-2011

| Year | Maximum Tax Rate (1) | Effective Tax Rate $250,000 Taxable Income (2) | Employment (3) (thousands) | | |
|------|------|------|------|------|------|
| | | | Increase (Decrease) | Increase | (Decrease) |
| 1983 | 50.0% | 43.6% | 4,040 | 4,040 | |
| 1984 | 50.0% | 42.6% | 3,101 | 3,101 | |
| 1985 | 50.0% | 42.3% | 2,585 | 2,585 | |
| 1986 | 50.0% | 42.0% | 2,066 | 2,066 | |
| 1987 | 38.5% | 34.5% | 3,063 | 3,063 | |
| 1988* | 28.0% | 28.5% | 2,692 | 2,692 | |
| 1989* | 28.0% | 28.5% | 2,373 | 2,373 | |
| 1990* | 28.0% | 28.5% | (1,141) | | (1,141) |
| 1991 | 31.0% | 28.2% | 38 | 38 | |
| 1992 | 31.0% | 28.1% | 1,097 | 1,097 | |
| 1993 | 39.6% | 30.2% | 2,891 | 2,891 | |
| 1994 | 39.6% | 30.1% | 2,697 | 2,697 | |
| 1995 | 39.6% | 30.0% | 462 | 462 | |
| 1996 | 39.6% | 29.8% | 3,173 | 3,173 | |
| 1997 | 39.6% | 29.6% | 2,428 | 2,428 | |
| 1998 | 39.6% | 29.5% | 2,301 | 2,301 | |
| 1999 | 39.6% | 29.3% | 3,532 | 3,532 | |
| 2000 | 39.6% | 29.2% | 1,219 | 1,219 | |
| 2001 | 39.1% | 28.6% | (2,077) | | (2,077) |
| 2002 | 38.6% | 27.7% | 1,716 | 1,716 | |
| 2003 | 35.0% | 25.6% | 1,055 | 1,055 | |
| 2004 | 35.0% | 25.4% | 1,773 | 1,773 | |
| 2005 | 35.0% | 25.2% | 2,905 | 2,905 | |
| 2006 | 35.0% | 25.0% | 2,878 | 2,878 | |
| 2007 | 35.0% | 24.7% | 369 | 369 | |
| 2008 | 35.0% | 24.5% | (4,210) | | (4,210) |
| 2009 | 35.0% | 24.1% | (3,687) | | (3,687) |
| 2010 | 35.0% | 24.1% | 830 | 830 | |
| 2011 | 35.0% | 24.0% | 2,307 | 2,307 | |

(1) See Appendix B 1.1
(2) See Appendix B 5.2
(3) See Appendix C 1.1
* See Appendix B 5.3 for impact of surcharges and credit

## Maximum and Effective Income Tax Rates - $250,000 Taxable Income
### Comparison to Employment Increases (Decreases)
### 1953-2011

| Year | Maximum Tax Rate (1) | Effective Tax Rate $250,000 Taxable Income (2) | Employment (3) (thousands) Increase (Decrease) | Increase | (Decrease) |
|---|---|---|---|---|---|
| 2011 | 35.0% | 24.0% | 2,307 | 2,307 | |
| 2010 | 35.0% | 24.1% | 830 | 830 | |
| 2009 | 35.0% | 24.1% | (3,687) | | (3,687) |
| 2008 | 35.0% | 24.5% | (4,210) | | (4,210) |
| 2007 | 35.0% | 24.7% | 369 | 369 | |
| 2006 | 35.0% | 25.0% | 2,878 | 2,878 | |
| 2005 | 35.0% | 25.2% | 2,905 | 2,905 | |
| 2004 | 35.0% | 25.4% | 1,773 | 1,773 | |
| 2003 | 35.0% | 25.6% | 1,055 | 1,055 | |
| 9 | 35.0% | 24.7% | 469 | 12,117 | (7,897) |
| 2002 | 38.6% | 27.7% | 1,716 | 1,716 | |
| 1992 | 31.0% | 28.1% | 1,097 | 1,097 | |
| 1991 | 31.0% | 28.2% | 38 | 38 | |
| 1988* | 28.0% | 28.5% | 2,692 | 2,692 | |
| 1989* | 28.0% | 28.5% | 2,373 | 2,373 | |
| 1990* | 28.0% | 28.5% | (1,141) | | (1,141) |
| 2001 | 39.1% | 28.6% | (2,077) | | (2,077) |
| 7 | 32.0% | 28.3% | 671 | 7,916 | (3,218) |
| 2000 | 39.6% | 29.2% | 1,219 | 1,219 | |
| 1999 | 39.6% | 29.3% | 3,532 | 3,532 | |
| 1998 | 39.6% | 29.5% | 2,301 | 2,301 | |
| 1997 | 39.6% | 29.6% | 2,428 | 2,428 | |
| 1996 | 39.6% | 29.8% | 3,173 | 3,173 | |
| 1995 | 39.6% | 30.0% | 462 | 462 | |
| 1994 | 39.6% | 30.1% | 2,697 | 2,697 | |
| 1993 | 39.6% | 30.2% | 2,891 | 2,891 | |
| 1987 | 38.5% | 34.5% | 3,063 | 3,063 | |
| 9 | 39.5% | 30.2% | 2,418 | 21,766 | 0 |
| 1986 | 50.0% | 42.0% | 2,066 | 2,066 | |
| 1985 | 50.0% | 42.3% | 2,585 | 2,585 | |
| 1984 | 50.0% | 42.6% | 3,101 | 3,101 | |
| 1983 | 50.0% | 43.6% | 4,040 | 4,040 | |
| 1982 | 50.0% | 45.0% | (531) | | (531) |
| 5 | 50.0% | 43.1% | 2,252 | 11,792 | (531) |

(1) See Appendix B 1.1     (2) See Appendices A 7.1 and A 7.2
(3) See Appendix C 1.1
* See Appendix B 5.3 for impact of surcharges and credit

Maximum and Effective Income Tax Rates - $250,000 Taxable Income
Comparison to Employment Increases (Decreases)
1953-2011

| Year | Maximum Tax Rate (1) | Effective Tax Rate $250,000 Taxable Income (2) | Employment (3) (thousands) | | |
|---|---|---|---|---|---|
| | | | Increase (Decrease) | Increase | (Decrease) |
| 1981* | 70.0% | 56.0% | (263) | | (263) |
| 1979 | 70.0% | 56.7% | 1,931 | 1,931 | |
| 1980 | 70.0% | 56.7% | 76 | 76 | |
| 1977 | 70.0% | 57.7% | 4,456 | 4,456 | |
| 1978 | 70.0% | 57.7% | 3,564 | 3,564 | |
| 1965 | 70.0% | 58.4% | 2,201 | 2,201 | |
| 1966 | 70.0% | 58.4% | 1,473 | 1,473 | |
| 1967 | 70.0% | 58.4% | 1,029 | 1,029 | |
| 1971 | 70.0% | 58.4% | 2,095 | 2,095 | |
| 1972 | 70.0% | 58.4% | 2,202 | 2,202 | |
| 1973 | 70.0% | 58.4% | 3,394 | 3,394 | |
| 1974 | 70.0% | 58.4% | (928) | | (928) |
| 1975 | 70.0% | 58.4% | 1,773 | 1,773 | |
| 1976 | 70.0% | 58.4% | 2,528 | 2,528 | |
| 1970* | 70.0% | 59.9% | 84 | 84 | |
| 1968* | 70.0% | 62.8% | 2,105 | 2,105 | |
| 1964 | 77.0% | 62.8% | 1,670 | 1,670 | |
| 1969* | 70.0% | 64.2% | 1,975 | 1,975 | |
| 18 | 70.4% | 58.9% | 1,743 | 32,556 | (1,191) |
| 1955 | 91.0% | 71.7% | 3,000 | 3,000 | |
| 1956 | 91.0% | 71.7% | (121) | | (121) |
| 1957 | 91.0% | 71.7% | (412) | | (412) |
| 1958 | 91.0% | 71.7% | 648 | 648 | |
| 1959 | 91.0% | 71.7% | 1,479 | 1,479 | |
| 1960 | 91.0% | 71.7% | 429 | 429 | |
| 1961 | 91.0% | 71.7% | 332 | 332 | |
| 1962 | 91.0% | 71.7% | 964 | 964 | |
| 1963 | 91.0% | 71.7% | 1,255 | 1,255 | |
| 1954 | 91.0% | 80.9% | 729 | 729 | |
| 1953 | 92.0% | 82.7% | (1,576) | | (1,576) |
| 11 | 91.1% | 73.5% | 612 | 8,836 | (2,109) |

(1) See Appendix B 1.1
(2) See Appendices A 7.1 and A 7.2
(3) See Appendix C 1.1
* See Appendix B 5.3 for impact of surcharges and credit

### Change in Effective Income Tax Rates - $250,000 Taxable Income
### Comparison to Employment Increases (Decreases)
### 1953-1982

| Year | Maximum Tax Rate (1) | Effective Tax Rate $250,000 Taxable Income (2) | Change in Effective Tax Rate (3) | Employment Increase (Decrease) (thousands) (4) |
|------|------|------|------|------|
| 1953 | 92.0% | 82.7% | 0.0% | (1,576) |
| 1954 | 91.0% | 80.9% | -1.8% | 729 |
| 1955 | 91.0% | 71.7% | -9.3% | 3,000 |
| 1956 | 91.0% | 71.7% | 0.0% | (121) |
| 1957 | 91.0% | 71.7% | 0.0% | (412) |
| 1958 | 91.0% | 71.7% | 0.0% | 648 |
| 1959 | 91.0% | 71.7% | 0.0% | 1,479 |
| 1960 | 91.0% | 71.7% | 0.0% | 429 |
| 1961 | 91.0% | 71.7% | 0.0% | 332 |
| 1962 | 91.0% | 71.7% | 0.0% | 964 |
| 1963 | 91.0% | 71.7% | 0.0% | 1,255 |
| 1964 | 77.0% | 62.8% | -8.9% | 1,670 |
| 1965 | 70.0% | 58.4% | -4.4% | 2,201 |
| 1966 | 70.0% | 58.4% | 0.0% | 1,473 |
| 1967 | 70.0% | 58.4% | 0.0% | 1,029 |
| 1968* | 70.0% | 62.8% | 4.4% | 2,105 |
| 1969* | 70.0% | 64.2% | 1.5% | 1,975 |
| 1970* | 70.0% | 59.9% | -4.4% | 84 |
| 1971 | 70.0% | 58.4% | -1.5% | 2,095 |
| 1972 | 70.0% | 58.4% | 0.0% | 2,202 |
| 1973 | 70.0% | 58.4% | 0.0% | 3,394 |
| 1974 | 70.0% | 58.4% | 0.0% | (928) |
| 1975 | 70.0% | 58.4% | 0.0% | 1,773 |
| 1976 | 70.0% | 58.4% | 0.0% | 2,528 |
| 1977 | 70.0% | 57.7% | -0.6% | 4,456 |
| 1978 | 70.0% | 57.7% | 0.0% | 3,564 |
| 1979 | 70.0% | 56.7% | -1.1% | 1,931 |
| 1980 | 70.0% | 56.7% | 0.0% | 76 |
| 1981* | 70.0% | 56.0% | -0.7% | (263) |
| 1982 | 50.0% | 45.0% | -11.0% | (531) |

(1) See Appendix B 1.1
(2) See Appendix B 5.1
(3) Effective tax rate in each year - Effective tax rate the preceding year
(4) See Appendix C 1.1
\* See Appendix B 5.3 for impact of surcharges and credit

## Change in Effective Income Tax Rates - $250,000 Taxable Income
## Comparison to Employment Increases (Decreases)
### 1983-2011

| Year | Maximum Tax Rate (1) | Effective Tax Rate $250,000 Taxable Income (2) | Change in Effective Tax Rate (3) | Employment Increase (Decrease) (thousands) (4) |
|---|---|---|---|---|
| 1983 | 50.0% | 43.6% | -1.38% | 4,040 |
| 1984 | 50.0% | 42.6% | -1.04% | 3,101 |
| 1985 | 50.0% | 42.3% | -0.30% | 2,585 |
| 1986 | 50.0% | 42.0% | -0.29% | 2,066 |
| 1987 | 38.5% | 34.5% | -7.50% | 3,063 |
| 1988* | 28.0% | 28.5% | -5.94% | 2,692 |
| 1989* | 28.0% | 28.5% | 0.01% | 2,373 |
| 1990* | 28.0% | 28.5% | -0.09% | (1,141) |
| 1991 | 31.0% | 28.2% | -0.21% | 38 |
| 1992 | 31.0% | 28.1% | -0.15% | 1,097 |
| 1993 | 39.6% | 30.2% | 2.11% | 2,891 |
| 1994 | 39.6% | 30.1% | -0.09% | 2,697 |
| 1995 | 39.6% | 30.0% | -0.15% | 462 |
| 1996 | 39.6% | 29.8% | -0.17% | 3,173 |
| 1997 | 39.6% | 29.6% | -0.17% | 2,428 |
| 1998 | 39.6% | 29.5% | -0.18% | 2,301 |
| 1999 | 39.6% | 29.3% | -0.11% | 3,532 |
| 2000 | 39.6% | 29.2% | -0.12% | 1,219 |
| 2001 | 39.1% | 28.6% | -0.62% | (2,077) |
| 2002 | 38.6% | 27.7% | -0.87% | 1,716 |
| 2003 | 35.0% | 25.6% | -2.15% | 1,055 |
| 2004 | 35.0% | 25.4% | -0.17% | 1,773 |
| 2005 | 35.0% | 25.2% | -0.17% | 2,905 |
| 2006 | 35.0% | 25.0% | -0.24% | 2,878 |
| 2007 | 35.0% | 24.7% | -0.31% | 369 |
| 2008 | 35.0% | 24.5% | -0.19% | (4,210) |
| 2009 | 35.0% | 24.1% | -0.36% | (3,687) |
| 2010 | 35.0% | 24.1% | -0.02% | 830 |
| 2011 | 35.0% | 24.0% | -0.13% | 2,307 |

(1) See Appendix B 1.1
(2) See Appendix B 5.2
(3) Effective tax rate in each year - Effective tax rate the preceding year
(4) See Appendix C 1.1
* See Appendix B 5.3 for impact of surcharges and credit

### Change in Effective Income Tax Rates - $250,000 Taxable Income
### Comparison to Employment Increases (Decreases)
### By Change in Effective Tax Rate
### 1953-2011

| Year | Maximum Tax Rate (1) | Effective Tax Rate $250,000 Taxable Income (2) | Change in Effective Tax Rate (2) | Employment Increase (Decrease) (thousands) (3) |
|------|------|------|------|------|
| 1982 | 50.0% | 45.0% | -11.00% | (531) |
| 1955 | 91.0% | 71.7% | -9.27% | 3,000 |
| 1964 | 77.0% | 62.8% | -8.88% | 1,670 |
| 1987 | 38.5% | 34.5% | -7.50% | 3,063 |
| 1988* | 28.0% | 28.5% | -6.04% | 2,692 |
| 1965 | 70.0% | 58.4% | -4.38% | 2,201 |
| 1970* | 70.0% | 59.9% | -4.38% | 84 |
| 2003 | 35.0% | 25.6% | -2.15% | 1,055 |
| 1954 | 91.0% | 80.9% | -1.76% | 729 |
| 1971 | 70.0% | 58.4% | -1.46% | 2,095 |
| 1983 | 50.0% | 43.6% | -1.38% | 4,040 |
| 1979 | 70.0% | 56.7% | -1.06% | 1,931 |
| 1984 | 50.0% | 42.6% | -1.04% | 3,101 |
| 2002 | 38.6% | 27.7% | -0.87% | 1,716 |
| 1981* | 70.0% | 56.0% | -0.71% | (263) |
| 1977 | 70.0% | 57.7% | -0.64% | 4,456 |
| 2001 | 39.1% | 28.6% | -0.62% | (2,077) |
| 1994 | 39.6% | 30.1% | -0.49% | 2,697 |
| 2009 | 35.0% | 24.1% | -0.36% | (3,687) |
| 2007 | 35.0% | 24.7% | -0.31% | 369 |
| 1985 | 50.0% | 42.3% | -0.30% | 2,585 |
| 1986 | 50.0% | 42.0% | -0.29% | 2,066 |
| 2006 | 35.0% | 25.0% | -0.24% | 2,878 |
| 1991 | 31.0% | 28.2% | -0.21% | 38 |
| 2008 | 35.0% | 24.5% | -0.19% | (4,210) |
| 1998 | 39.6% | 29.5% | -0.18% | 2,301 |
| 2005 | 35.0% | 25.2% | -0.17% | 2,905 |
| 1996 | 39.6% | 29.8% | -0.17% | 3,173 |
| 1997 | 39.6% | 29.6% | -0.17% | 2,428 |
| 2004 | 35.0% | 25.4% | -0.17% | 1,773 |

(1) See Appendix B 1.1
(2) See Appendices A 8.1 and A 8.2
(3) See Appendix C 1.1
* See Appendix B 5.3 for impact of surcharges and credit

Change in Effective Income Tax Rates - $250,000 Taxable Income
Comparison to Employment Increases (Decreases)
By Change in Effective Tax Rate
1953-2011

| Year | Maximum Income Tax Rate (1) | Effective Tax Rate $250,000 Taxable Income (2) | Change in Effective Tax Rate (2) | Employment Increase (Decrease) (thousands) (3) |
|---|---|---|---|---|
| 1995 | 39.6% | 30.0% | -0.15% | 462 |
| 1992 | 31.0% | 28.1% | -0.15% | 1,097 |
| 2011 | 35.0% | 24.0% | -0.13% | 2,307 |
| 2000 | 39.6% | 29.2% | -0.12% | 1,219 |
| 1999 | 39.6% | 29.3% | -0.11% | 3,532 |
| 2010 | 35.0% | 24.1% | -0.02% | 830 |
| 1953 | 92.0% | 82.7% | 0.00% | (1,576) |
| 1956 | 91.0% | 71.7% | 0.00% | (121) |
| 1957 | 91.0% | 71.7% | 0.00% | (412) |
| 1958 | 91.0% | 71.7% | 0.00% | 648 |
| 1959 | 91.0% | 71.7% | 0.00% | 1,479 |
| 1960 | 91.0% | 71.7% | 0.00% | 429 |
| 1961 | 91.0% | 71.7% | 0.00% | 332 |
| 1962 | 91.0% | 71.7% | 0.00% | 964 |
| 1963 | 91.0% | 71.7% | 0.00% | 1,255 |
| 1966 | 70.0% | 58.4% | 0.00% | 1,473 |
| 1967 | 70.0% | 58.4% | 0.00% | 1,029 |
| 1972 | 70.0% | 58.4% | 0.00% | 2,202 |
| 1973 | 70.0% | 58.4% | 0.00% | 3,394 |
| 1974 | 70.0% | 58.4% | 0.00% | (928) |
| 1975 | 70.0% | 58.4% | 0.00% | 1,773 |
| 1976 | 70.0% | 58.4% | 0.00% | 2,528 |
| 1978 | 70.0% | 57.7% | 0.00% | 3,564 |
| 1980 | 70.0% | 56.7% | 0.00% | 76 |
| 1990* | 28.0% | 28.5% | 0.01% | (1,141) |
| 1989* | 28.0% | 28.5% | 0.01% | 2,373 |
| 1969* | 70.0% | 64.2% | 1.46% | 1,975 |
| 1993 | 39.6% | 30.2% | 2.51% | 2,891 |
| 1968* | 70.0% | 62.8% | 4.38% | 2,105 |

(1) See Appendix B 1.1
(2) See Appendices A 8.1 and A 8.2
(3) See Appendix C 1.1
* See Appendix B 5.3 for impact of surcharges and credit

### Change in Effective Income Tax Rates - $250,000 Taxable Income 1953-2011
### Result of Decreases and Increases in Effective Tax Rate
### Comparison to Employment Increases (Decreases)

| Year | Maximum Tax Rate (1) | Effective Tax Rate $250,000 Taxable Income (2) | Change in Effective Tax Rate (2) | Employment (3) (thousands) Increase (Decrease) | Increase | (Decrease) |
|------|------|------|------|------|------|------|
| 1982 | 50.0% | 45.0% | | -11.0% | (531) | (531) | |
| 1955 | 91.0% | 71.7% | | -9.3% | 3,000 | 3,000 | |
| 1964 | 77.0% | 62.8% | | -8.9% | 1,670 | 1,670 | |
| 1987 | 38.5% | 34.5% | | -7.5% | 3,063 | 3,063 | |
| 1988* | 28.0% | 28.5% | (a) | -6.0% | 2,692 | 2,692 | |
| 1965 | 70.0% | 58.4% | | -4.4% | 2,201 | 2,201 | |
| 1970* | 70.0% | 59.9% | (b) | -4.4% | 84 | 84 | |
| 2003 | 35.0% | 25.6% | | -2.1% | 1,055 | 1,055 | |
| 1954 | 91.0% | 80.9% | | -1.8% | 729 | 729 | |
| 1971 | 70.0% | 58.4% | (c) | -1.5% | 2,095 | 2,095 | |
| 1979 | 70.0% | 56.7% | | -1.1% | 1,931 | 1,931 | |
| 2002 | 38.6% | 27.7% | | -0.9% | 1,716 | 1,716 | |
| 1981 | 70.0% | 56.0% | (d) | -0.7% | (263) | (263) | |
| 1977 | 70.0% | 57.7% | | -0.6% | 4,456 | 4,456 | |
| 2001 | 39.1% | 28.6% | | -0.6% | (2,077) | (2,077) | |
| 1991 | 31.0% | 28.2% | | -0.2% | 38 | 38 | |
| 1969* | 70.0% | 64.2% | (e) | 1.5% | 1,975 | | 1,975 |
| 1993 | 39.6% | 30.2% | | 2.5% | 2,891 | | 2,891 |
| 1968* | 70.0% | 62.8% | (f) | 4.4% | 2,105 | | 2,105 |
| | | Total | | | 28,830 | 21,859 | 6,971 |
| | | Average | | | 1,442 | 1,286 | 2,324 |

(1) See Appendix B 1.1

(2) See Appendices A 8.1 and A 8.2

(3) See Appendix C 1.1

(a) Reflect surcharge of lesser of 5% or exemptions

(b) Reflects reduction in surcharge from 10% to 2.5%

(c) Reflects elimination of surcharge

(d) Reflects credit of 1.25% on calculated tax

(e) Reflects surcharge of 7.5%

(e) Reflects surcharge of 10%

* See Appendix B 5.3 for impact of surcharges and credit

## Change in Effective Income Tax Rates - $250,000 Taxable Income
### Result of Inflation Adjustments 1953-2011
### Comparison to Employment Increases (Decreases)

| Year | Maximum Tax Rate (1) | Effective Tax Rate $250,000 Taxable Income (2) | Change in Effective Tax Rate (2) | Employment (3) (thousands) Increase (Decrease) | Increase | Decrease |
|---|---|---|---|---|---|---|
| 2011 | 35.0% | 24.0% | -0.13% | 2,307 | 2,307 | |
| 2009 | 35.0% | 24.1% | -0.36% | (3,687) | | (3,687) |
| 2008 | 35.0% | 24.5% | -0.19% | (4,210) | | (4,210) |
| 2007 | 35.0% | 24.7% | -0.31% | 369 | 369 | |
| 2006 | 35.0% | 25.0% | -0.24% | 2,878 | 2,878 | |
| 2005 | 35.0% | 25.2% | -0.17% | 2,905 | 2,905 | |
| 2004 | 35.0% | 25.4% | -0.17% | 1,773 | 1,773 | |
| 2010 | 35.0% | 24.1% | -0.02% | 830 | 830 | |
| 8 | 30.6% | 21.6% | -0.20% | 292 | 1,279 | (987) |
| 1992 | 31.0% | 28.1% | -0.15% | 1,097 | 1,097 | |
| 1989* | 28.0% | 28.5% | 0.01% | 2,373 | 2,373 | |
| 1990* | 28.0% | 28.5% | -0.09% | (1,141) | | (1,141) |
| 2000 | 39.6% | 29.2% | -0.12% | 1,219 | 1,219 | |
| 1999 | 39.6% | 29.3% | -0.11% | 3,532 | 3,532 | |
| 1998 | 39.6% | 29.5% | -0.18% | 2,301 | 2,301 | |
| 1997 | 39.6% | 29.6% | -0.17% | 2,428 | 2,428 | |
| 1996 | 39.6% | 29.8% | -0.17% | 3,173 | 3,173 | |
| 1995 | 39.6% | 30.0% | -0.15% | 462 | 462 | |
| 1994 | 39.6% | 30.1% | -0.49% | 2,697 | 2,697 | |
| 10 | 36.4% | 29.3% | -0.16% | 1,814 | 19,282 | (1,141) |
| 1986 | 50.0% | 42.0% | -0.29% | 2,066 | 2,066 | |
| 1985 | 50.0% | 42.3% | -0.30% | 2,585 | 2,585 | |
| 1984 | 50.0% | 42.6% | -1.04% | 3,101 | 3,101 | |
| 1983 | 50.0% | 43.6% | -1.38% | 4,040 | 4,040 | |
| 4 | 25.0% | 21.1% | -0.15% | 1,163 | 4,651 | 0 |
| | | | Total | 33,098 | 42,136 | (9,038) |
| | | | Average | 1,504 | 1,915 | (411) |

(1) See Appendix B 1.1
(2) See Appendices A 8.1 and A 8.2
(3) See Appendix C 1.1
* See Appendix B 5.3 for impact of surcharges and credit

## No Change in Effective Income Tax Rates 1953-2011
### Based on $250,000 Taxable Income
### Comparison to Employment Increases (Decreases)

| Year | Maximum Tax Rate (1) | Effective Tax Rate $250,000 Taxable Income (2) | Employment (3) (thousands) | | |
|---|---|---|---|---|---|
| | | | Increase (Decrease) | Increase | Decrease |
| 1980 | 70.0% | 56.7% | 76 | 76 | |
| 1978 | 70.0% | 57.7% | 3,564 | 3,564 | |
| 1966 | 70.0% | 58.4% | 1,473 | 1,473 | |
| 1967 | 70.0% | 58.4% | 1,029 | 1,029 | |
| 1972 | 70.0% | 58.4% | 2,202 | 2,202 | |
| 1973 | 70.0% | 58.4% | 3,394 | 3,394 | |
| 1974 | 70.0% | 58.4% | (928) | | (928) |
| 1975 | 70.0% | 58.4% | 1,773 | 1,773 | |
| 1976 | 70.0% | 58.4% | 2,528 | 2,528 | |
| 9 | 70.0% | 58.1% | 15,111 | 16,039 | (928) |
| 1956 | 91.0% | 71.7% | (121) | | (121) |
| 1957 | 91.0% | 71.7% | (412) | | (412) |
| 1958 | 91.0% | 71.7% | 648 | 648 | |
| 1959 | 91.0% | 71.7% | 1,479 | 1,479 | |
| 1960 | 91.0% | 71.7% | 429 | 429 | |
| 1961 | 91.0% | 71.7% | 332 | 332 | |
| 1962 | 91.0% | 71.7% | 964 | 964 | |
| 1963 | 91.0% | 71.7% | 1,255 | 1,255 | |
| 1953 | 92.0% | 82.7% | (1,576) | | (1,576) |
| 9 | 91.1% | 72.9% | 2,998 | 5,107 | (2,109) |
| | | Total | 18,109 | 21,146 | (3,037) |
| | | Average | 1,006 | 1,175 | (169) |

(1) See Appendix B 1.1

(2) See Appendices A 8.1 and A 8.2

(3) See Appendix C 1.1

*  See Appendix B 5.3 for impact of surcharges and credit

Capital Gains Tax Rates
Comparison to Employment Increases and Decreases
1953 - 2011
Sorted by Year

| Year | Capital Gains Tax Rate (1) | Employment Increase (2) (Decrease) (thousands) | Year | Capital Gains Tax Rate (1) | Employment Increase (2) (Decrease) (thousands) |
|---|---|---|---|---|---|
| 1953 | 25.00% | (1,576) | 1983 | 20.00% | 4,040 |
| 1954 | 25.00% | 729 | 1984 | 20.00% | 3,101 |
| 1955 | 25.00% | 3,000 | 1985 | 20.00% | 2,585 |
| 1956 | 25.00% | (121) | 1986 | 20.00% | 2,066 |
| 1957 | 25.00% | (412) | 1987 | 28.00% | 3,063 |
| 1958 | 25.00% | 648 | 1988 | 33.00% | 2,692 |
| 1959 | 25.00% | 1,479 | 1989 | 33.00% | 2,373 |
| 1960 | 25.00% | 429 | 1990 | 28.00% | (1,141) |
| 1961 | 25.00% | 332 | 1991 | 28.00% | 38 |
| 1962 | 25.00% | 964 | 1992 | 28.00% | 1,097 |
| 1963 | 25.00% | 1,255 | 1993 | 28.00% | 2,891 |
| 1964 | 25.00% | 1,670 | 1994 | 28.00% | 2,697 |
| 1965 | 25.00% | 2,201 | 1995 | 28.00% | 462 |
| 1966 | 25.00% | 1,473 | 1996 | 28.00% | 3,173 |
| 1967 | 25.00% | 1,029 | 1997 | 28.00% | 2,428 |
| 1968 | 26.90% | 2,105 | 1998 | 28.00% | 2,301 |
| 1969 | 27.50% | 1,975 | 1999 | 28.00% | 3,532 |
| 1970 | 32.30% | 84 | 2000 | 20.00% | 1,219 |
| 1971 | 34.30% | 2,095 | 2001 | 20.00% | (2,077) |
| 1972 | 36.50% | 2,202 | 2002 | 20.00% | 1,716 |
| 1973 | 36.50% | 3,394 | 2003 | 15.00% | 1,055 |
| 1974 | 36.50% | (928) | 2004 | 15.00% | 1,773 |
| 1975 | 36.50% | 1,773 | 2005 | 15.00% | 2,905 |
| 1976 | 39.90% | 2,528 | 2006 | 15.00% | 2,878 |
| 1977 | 39.90% | 4,456 | 2007 | 15.00% | 369 |
| 1978 | 39.00% | 3,564 | 2008 | 15.00% | (4,210) |
| 1979 | 28.00% | 1,931 | 2009 | 15.00% | (3,687) |
| 1980 | 28.00% | 76 | 2010 | 15.00% | 830 |
| 1981 | 23.70% | (263) | 2011 | 15.00% | 2,307 |
| 1982 | 20.00% | (531) | | | |

(1) See Appendix B 9.0
(2) See Appendix C 1.1

## Capital Gains Tax Rates
### Comparison to Employment Increases and Decreases
### 1953 - 2011
### Sorted by Capital Gains Rate

| Year | Capital Gains Tax Rate (1) | Employment (2) (thousands) Increase (Decrease) | Increase | (Decrease) |
|------|------|------|------|------|
| 2003 | 15.0% | 1,055 | 1,055 | |
| 2004 | 15.0% | 1,773 | 1,773 | |
| 2005 | 15.0% | 2,905 | 2,905 | |
| 2006 | 15.0% | 2,878 | 2,878 | |
| 2007 | 15.0% | 369 | 369 | |
| 2008 | 15.0% | (4,210) | | (4,210) |
| 2009 | 15.0% | (3,687) | | (3,687) |
| 2010 | 15.0% | 830 | 830 | |
| 2011 | 15.0% | 2,307 | 2,307 | |
| 9 | 15.0% | 4,220 | 12,117 | (7,897) |
| 1982 | 20.0% | (531) | | (531) |
| 1983 | 20.0% | 4,040 | 4,040 | |
| 1984 | 20.0% | 3,101 | 3,101 | |
| 1985 | 20.0% | 2,585 | 2,585 | |
| 1986 | 20.0% | 2,066 | 2,066 | |
| 2000 | 20.0% | 1,219 | 1,219 | |
| 2001 | 20.0% | (2,077) | | (2,077) |
| 2002 | 20.0% | 1,716 | 1,716 | |
| 8 | 20.0% | 12,119 | 14,727 | (2,608) |

(1) See Appendix B 9.0
(2) See Appendix C 1.1

## Capital Gains Tax Rates
### Comparison to Employment Increases and Decreases
### 1953 - 2011

Sorted by Capital Gains Rate

| Year | Capital Gains Tax Rate (1) | Employment (2) (thousands) | | |
|---|---|---|---|---|
| | | Increase (Decrease) | Increase | Decrease |
| 1981 | 23.7% | (263) | | (263) |
| 1953 | 25.0% | (1,576) | | (1,576) |
| 1954 | 25.0% | 729 | 729 | |
| 1955 | 25.0% | 3,000 | 3,000 | |
| 1956 | 25.0% | (121) | | (121) |
| 1957 | 25.0% | (412) | | (412) |
| 1958 | 25.0% | 648 | 648 | |
| 1959 | 25.0% | 1,479 | 1,479 | |
| 1960 | 25.0% | 429 | 429 | |
| 1961 | 25.0% | 332 | 332 | |
| 1962 | 25.0% | 964 | 964 | |
| 1963 | 25.0% | 1,255 | 1,255 | |
| 1964 | 25.0% | 1,670 | 1,670 | |
| 1965 | 25.0% | 2,201 | 2,201 | |
| 1966 | 25.0% | 1,473 | 1,473 | |
| 1967 | 25.0% | 1,029 | 1,029 | |
| 16 | 24.9% | 12,837 | 15,209 | (2,372) |

(1) See Appendix B 9.0
(2) See Appendix C 1.1

## Capital Gains Tax Rates
### Comparison to Employment Increases and Decreases
### 1953 - 2011
### Sorted by Capital Gains Rate

| Year | Capital Gains Tax Rate (1) | Employment (2) (thousands) Increase (Decrease) | Increase | Decrease |
|---|---|---|---|---|
| 1968 | 26.9% | 2,105 | 2,105 | |
| 1969 | 27.5% | 1,975 | 1,975 | |
| 1979 | 28.0% | 1,931 | 1,931 | |
| 1980 | 28.0% | 76 | 76 | |
| 1987 | 28.0% | 3,063 | 3,063 | |
| 1990 | 28.0% | (1,141) | | (1,141) |
| 1991 | 28.0% | 38 | 38 | |
| 1992 | 28.0% | 1,097 | 1,097 | |
| 1993 | 28.0% | 2,891 | 2,891 | |
| 1994 | 28.0% | 2,697 | 2,697 | |
| 1995 | 28.0% | 462 | 462 | |
| 1996 | 28.0% | 3,173 | 3,173 | |
| 1997 | 28.0% | 2,428 | 2,428 | |
| 1998 | 28.0% | 2,301 | 2,301 | |
| 1999 | 28.0% | 3,532 | 3,532 | |
| 15 | 27.9% | 26,628 | 27,769 | (1,141) |
| 1970 | 32.3% | 84 | 84 | |
| 1988 | 33.0% | 2,692 | 2,692 | |
| 1989 | 33.0% | 2,373 | 2,373 | |
| 1971 | 34.3% | 2,095 | 2,095 | |
| 4 | 33.2% | 7,244 | 7,244 | |
| 1972 | 36.5% | 2,202 | 2,202 | |
| 1973 | 36.5% | 3,394 | 3,394 | |
| 1974 | 36.5% | (928) | | (928) |
| 1975 | 36.5% | 1,773 | 1,773 | |
| 1978 | 39.0% | 3,564 | 3,564 | |
| 1976 | 39.9% | 2,528 | 2,528 | |
| 1977 | 39.9% | 4,456 | 4,456 | |
| 7 | 37.8% | 16,989 | 17,917 | (928) |

(1) See Appendix B 9.0
(2) See Appendix C 1.1

Corporate Income Tax Top Marginal Rates
Comparison to Employment Increases and Decreases
1953-2011
Sorted by Year

| Year | Corporate Income Tax Top Marginal Rate (1) | Employment Increase (2) (Decrease) (thousands) | Year | Corporate Income Tax Top Marginal Rate (1) | Employment Increase (2) (Decrease) (thousands) |
|---|---|---|---|---|---|
| 1953 | 52.00% | (1,576) | 1983 | 46.00% | 4,040 |
| 1954 | 52.00% | 729 | 1984 | 46.00% | 3,101 |
| 1955 | 52.00% | 3,000 | 1985 | 46.00% | 2,585 |
| 1956 | 52.00% | (121) | 1986 | 46.00% | 2,066 |
| 1957 | 52.00% | (412) | 1987 | 40.00% | 3,063 |
| 1958 | 52.00% | 648 | 1988 | 34.00% | 2,692 |
| 1959 | 52.00% | 1,479 | 1989 | 34.00% | 2,373 |
| 1960 | 52.00% | 429 | 1990 | 34.00% | (1,141) |
| 1961 | 52.00% | 332 | 1991 | 34.00% | 38 |
| 1962 | 52.00% | 964 | 1992 | 34.00% | 1,097 |
| 1963 | 52.00% | 1,255 | 1993 | 35.00% | 2,891 |
| 1964 | 50.00% | 1,670 | 1994 | 35.00% | 2,697 |
| 1965 | 48.00% | 2,201 | 1995 | 35.00% | 462 |
| 1966 | 48.00% | 1,473 | 1996 | 35.00% | 3,173 |
| 1967 | 48.00% | 1,029 | 1997 | 35.00% | 2,428 |
| 1968* | 52.80% | 2,105 | 1998 | 35.00% | 2,301 |
| 1969* | 52.80% | 1,975 | 1999 | 35.00% | 3,532 |
| 1970** | 49.20% | 84 | 2000 | 35.00% | 1,219 |
| 1971 | 48.00% | 2,095 | 2001 | 35.00% | (2,077) |
| 1972 | 48.00% | 2,202 | 2002 | 35.00% | 1,716 |
| 1973 | 48.00% | 3,394 | 2003 | 35.00% | 1,055 |
| 1974 | 48.00% | (928) | 2004 | 35.00% | 1,773 |
| 1975 | 48.00% | 1,773 | 2005 | 35.00% | 2,905 |
| 1976 | 48.00% | 2,528 | 2006 | 35.00% | 2,878 |
| 1977 | 48.00% | 4,456 | 2007 | 35.00% | 369 |
| 1978 | 48.00% | 3,564 | 2008 | 35.00% | (4,210) |
| 1979 | 46.00% | 1,931 | 2009 | 35.00% | (3,687) |
| 1980 | 46.00% | 76 | 2010 | 35.00% | 830 |
| 1981 | 46.00% | (263) | 2011 | 35.00% | 2,307 |
| 1982 | 46.00% | (531) | | | |

(1) See Appendix B 10.1
(2) See Appendix C 1.1
\* Reflects 10% surcharge
\*\* Reflects 2.5% surcharge

Corporate Income Tax Top Marginal Rates
Comparison to Employment Increases and Decreases
1953 -2011
Sorted by Rate

| Year | Corporate Income Tax Top Marginal Rate (1) | Employment (2) (thousands) | | |
|------|------|------|------|------|
| | | Increase (Decrease) | Increase | Decrease |
| 1988 | 34.00% | 2,692 | 2,692 | |
| 1989 | 34.00% | 2,373 | 2,373 | |
| 1990 | 34.00% | (1,141) | | (1,141) |
| 1991 | 34.00% | 38 | 38 | |
| 1992 | 34.00% | 1,097 | 1,097 | |
| 1993 | 35.00% | 2,891 | 2,891 | |
| 1994 | 35.00% | 2,697 | 2,697 | |
| 1995 | 35.00% | 462 | 462 | |
| 1996 | 35.00% | 3,173 | 3,173 | |
| 1997 | 35.00% | 2,428 | 2,428 | |
| 1998 | 35.00% | 2,301 | 2,301 | |
| 1999 | 35.00% | 3,532 | 3,532 | |
| 2000 | 35.00% | 1,219 | 1,219 | |
| 2001 | 35.00% | (2,077) | | (2,077) |
| 2002 | 35.00% | 1,716 | 1,716 | |
| 2003 | 35.00% | 1,055 | 1,055 | |
| 2004 | 35.00% | 1,773 | 1,773 | |
| 2005 | 35.00% | 2,905 | 2,905 | |
| 2006 | 35.00% | 2,878 | 2,878 | |
| 2007 | 35.00% | 369 | 369 | |
| 2008 | 35.00% | (4,210) | | (4,210) |
| 2009 | 35.00% | (3,687) | | (3,687) |
| 2010 | 35.00% | 830 | 830 | |
| 2011 | 35.00% | 2,307 | 2,307 | |
| 24 | 34.79% | 27,621 | 38,736 | (11,115) |

(1) See Appendix B 10.0
(2) See Appendix C 1.1

## Corporate Income Tax Top Marginal Rates
### Comparison to Employment Increases and Decreases
### 1953 -2011
### Sorted by Rate

| Year | Corporate Income Tax Top Marginal Rate (1) | Employment (2) (thousands) | | |
| --- | --- | --- | --- | --- |
| | | Increase (Decrease) | Increase | Decrease |
| 1987 | 40.00% | 3,063 | 3,063 | |
| 1979 | 46.00% | 1,931 | 1,931 | |
| 1980 | 46.00% | 76 | 76 | |
| 1981 | 46.00% | (263) | | (263) |
| 1982 | 46.00% | (531) | | (531) |
| 1983 | 46.00% | 4,040 | 4,040 | |
| 1984 | 46.00% | 3,101 | 3,101 | |
| 1985 | 46.00% | 2,585 | 2,585 | |
| 1986 | 46.00% | 2,066 | 2,066 | |
| 1965 | 48.00% | 2,201 | 2,201 | |
| 1966 | 48.00% | 1,473 | 1,473 | |
| 1967 | 48.00% | 1,029 | 1,029 | |
| 1971 | 48.00% | 2,095 | 2,095 | |
| 1972 | 48.00% | 2,202 | 2,202 | |
| 1973 | 48.00% | 3,394 | 3,394 | |
| 1974 | 48.00% | (928) | | (928) |
| 1975 | 48.00% | 1,773 | 1,773 | |
| 1976 | 48.00% | 2,528 | 2,528 | |
| 1977 | 48.00% | 4,456 | 4,456 | |
| 1978 | 48.00% | 3,564 | 3,564 | |
| 1970* | 49.20% | 84 | 84 | |
| 21 | 46.91% | 39,939 | 41,661 | (1,722) |

(1) See Appendix B 10.0
(2) See Appendix C 1.1

## Corporate Income Tax Top Marginal Rates
## Comparison to Employment Increases and Decreases
### 1953 -2011
#### Sorted by Rate

| Year | Corporate Income Tax Top Marginal Rate (1) | Employment (2) (thousands) | | |
| --- | --- | --- | --- | --- |
| | | Increase (Decrease) | Increase | Decrease |
| 1964 | 50.00% | 1,670 | 1,670 | |
| 1953 | 52.00% | (1,576) | | (1,576) |
| 1954 | 52.00% | 729 | 729 | |
| 1955 | 52.00% | 3,000 | 3,000 | |
| 1956 | 52.00% | (121) | | (121) |
| 1957 | 52.00% | (412) | | (412) |
| 1958 | 52.00% | 648 | 648 | |
| 1959 | 52.00% | 1,479 | 1,479 | |
| 1960 | 52.00% | 429 | 429 | |
| 1961 | 52.00% | 332 | 332 | |
| 1962 | 52.00% | 964 | 964 | |
| 1963 | 52.00% | 1,255 | 1,255 | |
| 1968* | 52.80% | 2,105 | 2,105 | |
| 1969* | 52.80% | 1,975 | 1,975 | |
| 14 | 51.97% | 12,477 | 14,586 | (2,109) |

(1) See Appendix B 10.0
(2) See Appendix C 1.1

## Maximum Income Tax Rates
### Comparison to Employment Increases and Decreases by Presidential Term
### 1953 - 2011

| Year | Net Change in Employed (!) | Maximum Income Tax Rates (2) | | Year | Net Change in Employed (!) | Maximum Income Tax Rates (2) |
|---|---|---|---|---|---|---|
| Eisenhower: Jan, 1953 - Jan, 1961 | | | | Nixon / Ford: Jan, 1969 - Jan, 1977 | | |
| 1953 | (1,576) | 92.0% | | 1969 | 1,975 | 70.0% |
| 1954 | 729 | 91.0% | | 1970 | 84 | 70.0% |
| 1955 | 3,000 | 91.0% | | 1971 | 2,095 | 70.0% |
| 1956 | (121) | 91.0% | | 1972 | 2,202 | 70.0% |
| 1957 | (412) | 91.0% | | 1973 | 3,394 | 70.0% |
| 1958 | 648 | 91.0% | | 1974 | (928) | 70.0% |
| 1959 | 1,479 | 91.0% | | 1975 | 1,773 | 70.0% |
| 1960 | 429 | 91.0% | | 1976 | 2,528 | 70.0% |
| Change | 4,176 | 91.1% | | Change | 13,123 | 70.0% |

| Year | Net Change in Employed (!) | Maximum Income Tax Rates (2) | | Year | Net Change in Employed (!) | Maximum Income Tax Rates (2) |
|---|---|---|---|---|---|---|
| Kennedy/Johnson: Jan, 1961- Jan, 1965 | | | | Carter: Jan, 1977 - Jan, 1981 | | |
| 1961 | 332 | 91.0% | | 1977 | 4,456 | 70.0% |
| 1962 | 964 | 91.0% | | 1978 | 3,564 | 70.0% |
| 1963 | 1,255 | 91.0% | | 1979 | 1,931 | 70.0% |
| 1964 | 1,670 | 77.0% | | 1980 | 76 | 70.0% |
| Change | 4,221 | 87.5% | | Change | 10,027 | 70.0% |

| Year | Net Change in Employed (!) | Maximum Income Tax Rates (2) | | Year | Net Change in Employed (!) | Maximum Income Tax Rates (2) |
|---|---|---|---|---|---|---|
| Johnson: Jan, 1965- Jan, 1969 | | | | Reagan: Jan, 1981 - Jan, 1989 | | |
| 1965 | 2,201 | 70.0% | | 1981 | (263) | 70.0% |
| 1966 | 1,473 | 70.0% | | 1982 | (531) | 50.0% |
| 1967 | 1,029 | 70.0% | | 1983 | 4,040 | 50.0% |
| 1968 | 2,105 | 70.0% | | 1984 | 3,101 | 50.0% |
| Change | 6,808 | 70.0% | | 1985 | 2,585 | 50.0% |
| | | | | 1986 | 2,066 | 50.0% |
| | | | | 1987 | 3,063 | 38.5% |
| | | | | 1988 | 2,692 | 28.0% |
| | | | | Change | 16,753 | 48.3% |

(1) See Appendix C 2.1
(2) See Appendices B 1.1 and B 1.2

# Maximum Income Tax Rates
## Comparison to Employment Increases and Decreases by Presidential Term
### 1989 - 2011

| Year | Net Change in Employed (!) | Maximum Income Tax Rates (2) |
|---|---|---|
| Bush (1): Jan, 1989 - Jan, 1993 | | |
| 1989 | 2,373 | 28.0% |
| 1990 | (1,141) | 28.0% |
| 1991 | 38 | 31.0% |
| 1992 | 1,097 | 31.0% |
| Change | 2,367 | 29.5% |

| Year | Net Change in Employed (!) | Maximum Income Tax Rates (2) |
|---|---|---|
| Obama: Jan, 2009 - | | |
| 2009 | (3,687) | 35.0% |
| 2010 | 830 | 35.0% |
| 2011 | 2,307 | 35.0% |
| Change | (550) | 35.0% |

| Clinton: Jan, 1993 - Jan, 2001 | | |
|---|---|---|
| 1993 | 2,891 | 39.6% |
| 1994 | 2,697 | 39.6% |
| 1995 | 462 | 39.6% |
| 1996 | 3,173 | 39.6% |
| 1997 | 2,428 | 39.6% |
| 1998 | 2,301 | 39.6% |
| 1999 | 3,532 | 39.6% |
| 2000 | 1,219 | 39.6% |
| Change | 18,703 | 39.6% |

| Bush (2): Jan, 2001 - Jan, 2009 | | |
|---|---|---|
| 2001 | (2,077) | 39.1% |
| 2002 | 1,716 | 38.6% |
| 2003 | 1,055 | 35.0% |
| 2004 | 1,773 | 35.0% |
| 2005 | 2,905 | 35.0% |
| 2006 | 2,878 | 35.0% |
| 2007 | 369 | 35.0% |
| 2008 | (4,210) | 35.0% |
| Change | 4,409 | 36.0% |

(1) See Appendix C 2.1

## Maximum Income Tax Rates
### Comparison to Employment Increases and Decreases by Presidential Term +/- One Year*
### 1954 - 1989

| Year | Net Change in Employed (!) | Maximum Income Tax Rates (2) | Year | Net Change in Employed (!) | Maximum Income Tax Rates (2) |
|---|---|---|---|---|---|
| Eisenhower: Jan, 1953 - Jan, 1961 | | | Nixon / Ford: Jan, 1969 - Jan, 1977 | | |
| 1954 | 729 | 92.0% | 1970 | 84 | 70.0% |
| 1955 | 3,000 | 91.0% | 1971 | 2,095 | 70.0% |
| 1956 | (121) | 91.0% | 1972 | 2,202 | 70.0% |
| 1957 | (412) | 91.0% | 1973 | 3,394 | 70.0% |
| 1958 | 648 | 91.0% | 1974 | (928) | 70.0% |
| 1959 | 1,479 | 91.0% | 1975 | 1,773 | 70.0% |
| 1960 | 429 | 91.0% | 1976 | 2,528 | 70.0% |
| 1961 | 332 | 91.0% | 1977 | 4,456 | 70.0% |
| Change | 6,084 | 91.1% | Change | 15,604 | 70.0% |

| Year | Net Change in Employed (!) | Maximum Income Tax Rates (2) | Year | Net Change in Employed (!) | Maximum Income Tax Rates (2) |
|---|---|---|---|---|---|
| Kennedy/Johnson: Jan, 1961- Jan, 1965 | | | Carter:  Jan, 1977 - Jan, 1981 | | |
| 1962 | 964 | 91.0% | 1978 | 3,564 | 70.0% |
| 1963 | 1,255 | 91.0% | 1979 | 1,931 | 70.0% |
| 1964 | 1,670 | 91.0% | 1980 | 76 | 70.0% |
| 1965 | 2,201 | 77.0% | 1981 | (263) | 70.0% |
| Change | 6,090 | 87.5% | Change | 5,308 | 70.0% |

| Year | Net Change in Employed (!) | Maximum Income Tax Rates (2) | Year | Net Change in Employed (!) | Maximum Income Tax Rates (2) |
|---|---|---|---|---|---|
| Johnson: Jan, 1965- Jan, 1969 | | | Reagan: Jan, 1981 - Jan, 1989 | | |
| 1966 | 1,473 | 70.0% | 1982 | (531) | 70.0% |
| 1967 | 1,029 | 70.0% | 1983 | 4,040 | 50.0% |
| 1968 | 2,105 | 70.0% | 1984 | 3,101 | 50.0% |
| 1969 | 1,975 | 70.0% | 1985 | 2,585 | 50.0% |
| Change | 6,582 | 70.0% | 1986 | 2,066 | 50.0% |
| | | | 1987 | 3,063 | 50.0% |
| | | | 1988 | 2,692 | 38.5% |
| | | | 1989 | 2,373 | 28.0% |
| | | | Change | 19,389 | 48.3% |

(1) See Appendix C 2.1

(2) See Appendices B 1.1 and B 1.2

* Beginning January one year after entering office and ending January one year after
  leaving office. Tax rates relate to previous year.

## Maximum Income Tax Rates
### Comparison to Employment Increases and Decreases by Presidential Term +/- One Year*
### 1990 - 2011

| Year | Net Change in Employed (!) | Maximum Income Tax Rates (2) |
|------|------|------|
| Bush (1): Jan, 1989 - Jan, 1993 | | |
| 1990 | (1,141) | 28.0% |
| 1991 | 38 | 28.0% |
| 1992 | 1,097 | 31.0% |
| 1993 | 2,891 | 31.0% |
| Change | 2,885 | 29.5% |

| Year | Net Change in Employed (!) | Maximum Income Tax Rates (2) |
|------|------|------|
| Obama: Jan, 2009 - | | |
| 2010 | 830 | 35.0% |
| 2011 | 2,307 | 35.0% |
| Change | 3,137 | 35.0% |

| Clinton: Jan, 1993 - Jan, 2001 | | |
|------|------|------|
| 1994 | 2,697 | 39.6% |
| 1995 | 462 | 39.6% |
| 1996 | 3,173 | 39.6% |
| 1997 | 2,428 | 39.6% |
| 1998 | 2,301 | 39.6% |
| 1999 | 3,532 | 39.6% |
| 2000 | 1,219 | 39.6% |
| 2001 | (2,077) | 39.6% |
| Change | 13,735 | 39.6% |

| Bush (2): Jan, 2001 - Jan, 2009 | | |
|------|------|------|
| 2002 | 1,716 | 39.1% |
| 2003 | 1,055 | 38.6% |
| 2004 | 1,773 | 35.0% |
| 2005 | 2,905 | 35.0% |
| 2006 | 2,878 | 35.0% |
| 2007 | 369 | 35.0% |
| 2008 | (4,210) | 35.0% |
| 2009 | (3,687) | 35.0% |
| Change | 2,799 | 36.0% |

(1) See Appendix C 2.1

(2) See Appendices B 1.1 and B 1.2

* Beginning January one year after entering office and ending January one year after leaving office. Tax rates relate to previous year.

## 2011 Taxes Based on $250,000 Taxable Income
## Deflated to Current Dollars in Selected Years
## 1955-2010

| Year | Bracket Rate At or Before 250000 (1) | Effective Tax rate (1) | Tax in Current Dollars (1) | 2011 Tax in Deflated Current Dollars (2) | Percentage Decrease in Current Taxes |
|------|------|------|------|------|------|
| 1955 | 89.00% | 71.66% | $179,140 | $8,783 | 95.10% |
| 1960 | 89.00% | 71.66% | $179,140 | $9,847 | 94.50% |
| 1965 | 70.00% | 58.39% | $145,980 | $10,547 | 92.78% |
| 1970 | 70.00% | 59.85% | $149,630 | $12,876 | 91.39% |
| 1975 | 70.00% | 58.39% | $145,980 | $17,771 | 87.83% |
| 1980 | 70.00% | 56.69% | $141,724 | $25,284 | 82.16% |
| 1985 | 50.00% | 42.26% | $104,928 | $32,604 | 68.93% |
| 1990 | 28.00% | 28.46% | $71,148 | $38,230 | 46.27% |
| 1995 | 36.00% | 29.97% | $74,923 | $43,173 | 42.38% |
| 2000 | 36.00% | 29.22% | $73,049 | $46,938 | 35.74% |
| 2005 | 33.00% | 25.24% | $63,092 | $52,904 | 16.15% |
| 2010 | 33.00% | 24.11% | $60,282 | $58,720 | 2.59% |
| 2011 | 33.00% | 23.98% | $59,955 | $59,955 | - |

(1) See Appendices B 5.1 and B 5.2

(2) See stats.areppim.com:
   Current to Real Dollars Converter (using GDP deflator)

## Maximum Individual Income Tax Rates and Taxable Income Brackets
### 1953-2011
#### (in current dollars)

| Year | Top Bracket | | | Year | Top Bracket | | |
|------|--------|---|-----------|------|--------|---|-----------|
|      | Rate * | | Amount    |      | Rate * | | Amount    |
| 1953 | 92.00% |     | $200,000 | 1983 | 50.00% |     | $109,400 |
| 1954 | 91.00% |     | $200,000 | 1984 | 50.00% |     | $162,400 |
| 1955 | 91.00% |     | $400,000 | 1985 | 50.00% |     | $169,020 |
| 1956 | 91.00% |     | $400,000 | 1986 | 50.00% |     | $175,250 |
| 1957 | 91.00% |     | $400,000 | 1987 | 38.50% |     | $90,000 |
| 1958 | 91.00% |     | $400,000 | 1988 | 28.00% | (5) | $149,250 |
| 1959 | 91.00% |     | $400,000 | 1989 | 28.00% | (5) | $155,320 |
| 1960 | 91.00% |     | $400,000 | 1990 | 28.00% | (5) | $162,770 |
| 1961 | 91.00% |     | $400,000 | 1991 | 31.00% |     | $82,150 |
| 1962 | 91.00% |     | $400,000 | 1992 | 31.00% |     | $86,500 |
| 1963 | 91.00% |     | $400,000 | 1993 | 39.60% |     | $250,000 |
| 1964 | 77.00% |     | $400,000 | 1994 | 39.60% |     | $250,000 |
| 1965 | 70.00% |     | $200,000 | 1995 | 39.60% |     | $256,500 |
| 1966 | 70.00% |     | $200,000 | 1996 | 39.60% |     | $263,750 |
| 1967 | 70.00% |     | $200,000 | 1997 | 39.60% |     | $271,050 |
| 1968 | 70.00% | (1) | $200,000 | 1998 | 39.60% |     | $278,450 |
| 1969 | 70.00% | (2) | $200,000 | 1999 | 39.60% |     | $283,150 |
| 1970 | 70.00% | (3) | $200,000 | 2000 | 39.60% |     | $288,350 |
| 1971 | 70.00% |     | $200,000 | 2001 | 39.10% |     | $297,350 |
| 1972 | 70.00% |     | $200,000 | 2002 | 38.60% |     | $307,050 |
| 1973 | 70.00% |     | $200,000 | 2003 | 35.00% |     | $311,950 |
| 1974 | 70.00% |     | $200,000 | 2004 | 35.00% |     | $319,100 |
| 1975 | 70.00% |     | $200,000 | 2005 | 35.00% |     | $326,450 |
| 1976 | 70.00% |     | $200,000 | 2006 | 35.00% |     | $336,550 |
| 1977 | 70.00% |     | $203,200 | 2007 | 35.00% |     | $349,700 |
| 1978 | 70.00% |     | $203,200 | 2008 | 35.00% |     | $357,700 |
| 1979 | 70.00% |     | $215,400 | 2009 | 35.00% |     | $372,950 |
| 1980 | 70.00% |     | $215,400 | 2010 | 35.00% |     | $373,650 |
| 1981 | 70.00% | (4) | $215,400 | 2011 | 35.00% |     | $379,150 |
| 1982 | 50.00% |     | $85,600  |      |        |     |          |

See Appendix B 1.2 for notes

Notes to Appendix B-1.1

Maximum Individual Income Tax Rates and Taxable Income Brackets

1953-2011

(in current dollars)


Source: Tax Rates: Internal Revenue Service Instructions to Form 1040 and Tax Rate
Tables of respective years - Married, filing jointly

* Rate at which income is taxed above Top Bracket Amount

Surcharge 1968-1970

(1)    Excludes 10% surcharge from April = 7.5% surcharge

(2)    Excludes 10% surcharge thru June=5% plus 5% thru December

(3)    Excludes 5%% surcharge thru June=2.5%

Credit 1981

(4)    Excludes from rate: 1.25% credit against calculated tax

Surcharge 1988-1990

(5)    Excludes surcharge of lesser of 5% of calculated tax or exemptions

## Changes in Maximum Individual Income Tax Rates
### 1953-2011
#### (in current dollars)

| Year | Maximum Tax Rate (1) | Change (2) | Year | Maximum Tax Rate (1) | Change (2) |
|------|------|------|------|------|------|
| 1953 | 92.00% | 0.0% | 1983 | 50.00% | 0.0% |
| 1954 | 91.00% | -1.0% | 1984 | 50.00% | 0.0% |
| 1955 | 91.00% | 0.0% | 1985 | 50.00% | 0.0% |
| 1956 | 91.00% | 0.0% | 1986 | 50.00% | 0.0% |
| 1957 | 91.00% | 0.0% | 1987 | 38.50% | -11.5% |
| 1958 | 91.00% | 0.0% | 1988 | 28.00% | -10.5% |
| 1959 | 91.00% | 0.0% | 1989 | 28.00% | 0.0% |
| 1960 | 91.00% | 0.0% | 1990 | 28.00% | 0.0% |
| 1961 | 91.00% | 0.0% | 1991 | 31.00% | 3.0% |
| 1962 | 91.00% | 0.0% | 1992 | 31.00% | 0.0% |
| 1963 | 91.00% | 0.0% | 1993 | 39.60% | 8.6% |
| 1964 | 77.00% | -14.0% | 1994 | 39.60% | 0.0% |
| 1965 | 70.00% | -7.0% | 1995 | 39.60% | 0.0% |
| 1966 | 70.00% | 0.0% | 1996 | 39.60% | 0.0% |
| 1967 | 70.00% | 0.0% | 1997 | 39.60% | 0.0% |
| 1968 | 70.00% | 0.0% | 1998 | 39.60% | 0.0% |
| 1969 | 70.00% | 0.0% | 1999 | 39.60% | 0.0% |
| 1970 | 70.00% | 0.0% | 2000 | 39.60% | 0.0% |
| 1971 | 70.00% | 0.0% | 2001 | 39.10% | -0.5% |
| 1972 | 70.00% | 0.0% | 2002 | 38.60% | -0.5% |
| 1973 | 70.00% | 0.0% | 2003 | 35.00% | -3.6% |
| 1974 | 70.00% | 0.0% | 2004 | 35.00% | 0.0% |
| 1975 | 70.00% | 0.0% | 2005 | 35.00% | 0.0% |
| 1976 | 70.00% | 0.0% | 2006 | 35.00% | 0.0% |
| 1977 | 70.00% | 0.0% | 2007 | 35.00% | 0.0% |
| 1978 | 70.00% | 0.0% | 2008 | 35.00% | 0.0% |
| 1979 | 70.00% | 0.0% | 2009 | 35.00% | 0.0% |
| 1980 | 70.00% | 0.0% | 2010 | 35.00% | 0.0% |
| 1981 | 70.00% | 0.0% | 2011 | 35.00% | 0.0% |
| 1982 | 50.00% | -20.0% | | | |

(1) See Appendix B 1.1

(2) Maximum tax rate in each year - Maximum tax rate the preceding year

### Individual Income Tax and Effective Tax Rates
### Taxable income of $1,000,000
### 1953-1982
### (in current dollars)

| Year | Top Bracket | | Tax at $1,000,000 | | Base Tax | Excess | Effective Tax Rate |
|---|---|---|---|---|---|---|---|
| | Rate * | Amount | Amount | | | | |
| 1953 | 92.00% | $200,000 | $896,716 | | $160,716 | $736,000 | 89.7% |
| 1954 | 91.00% | $200,000 | $884,820 | | $156,820 | $728,000 | 88.5% |
| 1955 | 91.00% | $400,000 | $859,640 | | $313,640 | $546,000 | 86.0% |
| 1956 | 91.00% | $400,000 | $859,640 | | $313,640 | $546,000 | 86.0% |
| 1957 | 91.00% | $400,000 | $859,640 | | $313,640 | $546,000 | 86.0% |
| 1958 | 91.00% | $400,000 | $859,640 | | $313,640 | $546,000 | 86.0% |
| 1959 | 91.00% | $400,000 | $859,640 | | $313,640 | $546,000 | 86.0% |
| 1960 | 91.00% | $400,000 | $859,640 | | $313,640 | $546,000 | 86.0% |
| 1961 | 91.00% | $400,000 | $859,640 | | $313,640 | $546,000 | 86.0% |
| 1962 | 91.00% | $400,000 | $859,640 | | $313,640 | $546,000 | 86.0% |
| 1963 | 91.00% | $400,000 | $859,640 | | $313,640 | $546,000 | 86.0% |
| 1964 | 77.00% | $400,000 | $733,680 | | $271,680 | $462,000 | 73.4% |
| 1965 | 70.00% | $200,000 | $670,980 | | $110,980 | $560,000 | 67.1% |
| 1966 | 70.00% | $200,000 | $670,980 | | $110,980 | $560,000 | 67.1% |
| 1967 | 70.00% | $200,000 | $670,980 | | $110,980 | $560,000 | 67.1% |
| 1968 | 70.00% | $200,000 | $721,304 | (1) | $110,980 | $560,000 | 72.1% |
| 1969 | 70.00% | $200,000 | $738,078 | (2) | $110,980 | $560,000 | 73.8% |
| 1970 | 70.00% | $200,000 | $687,755 | (3) | $110,980 | $560,000 | 68.8% |
| 1971 | 70.00% | $200,000 | $670,980 | | $110,980 | $560,000 | 67.1% |
| 1972 | 70.00% | $200,000 | $670,980 | | $110,980 | $560,000 | 67.1% |
| 1973 | 70.00% | $200,000 | $670,980 | | $110,980 | $560,000 | 67.1% |
| 1974 | 70.00% | $200,000 | $670,980 | | $110,980 | $560,000 | 67.1% |
| 1975 | 70.00% | $200,000 | $670,980 | | $110,980 | $560,000 | 67.1% |
| 1976 | 70.00% | $200,000 | $670,980 | | $110,980 | $560,000 | 67.1% |
| 1977 | 70.00% | $203,200 | $668,740 | | $110,980 | $557,760 | 66.9% |
| 1978 | 70.00% | $203,200 | $668,740 | | $110,980 | $557,760 | 66.9% |
| 1979 | 70.00% | $215,400 | $666,724 | | $117,504 | $549,220 | 66.7% |
| 1980 | 70.00% | $215,400 | $666,724 | | $117,504 | $549,220 | 66.7% |
| 1981 | 70.00% | $215,400 | $658,390 | (4) | $117,504 | $549,220 | 65.8% |
| 1982 | 50.00% | $85,600 | $487,449 | | $30,249 | $457,200 | 48.7% |

See Appendix B 3.3 for notes

## Individual Income Tax and Effective Tax Rates
### Taxable income of $1,000,000
### 1983-2011
### (in current dollars)

| Year | Top Bracket | | Tax at $1,000,000 | | Base Tax | Excess | Effective Tax Rate |
|------|-------------|--------|-------------------|-----|----------|--------|-------------------|
|      | Rate *      | Amount | Amount            |     | Tax      | Excess | Rate |
| 1983 | 50.00% | $109,400 | $484,002 |     | $38,702 | $445,300 | 48.40% |
| 1984 | 50.00% | $162,400 | $481,400 |     | $62,600 | $418,800 | 48.14% |
| 1985 | 50.00% | $169,020 | $480,642 |     | $65,152 | $415,490 | 48.06% |
| 1986 | 50.00% | $175,250 | $479,928 |     | $67,553 | $412,375 | 47.99% |
| 1987 | 38.50% | $90,000 | $374,940 |     | $24,590 | $350,350 | 37.49% |
| 1988 | 28.00% | $149,250 | $281,092 | (5) |         |          | 28.11% |
| 1989 | 28.00% | $155,320 | $281,120 | (6) |         |          | 28.11% |
| 1990 | 28.00% | $162,770 | $281,148 | (7) |         |          | 28.11% |
| 1991 | 31.00% | $82,150 | $303,116 |     | $18,582 | $284,534 | 30.31% |
| 1992 | 31.00% | $86,500 | $302,751 |     | $19,566 | $283,185 | 30.28% |
| 1993 | 39.60% | $250,000 | $372,529 |     | $75,529 | $297,000 | 37.25% |
| 1994 | 39.60% | $250,000 | $372,305 |     | $75,305 | $297,000 | 37.23% |
| 1995 | 39.60% | $256,500 | $371,689 |     | $77,263 | $294,426 | 37.17% |
| 1996 | 39.60% | $263,750 | $371,000 |     | $79,445 | $291,555 | 37.10% |
| 1997 | 39.60% | $271,050 | $370,311 |     | $81,647 | $288,664 | 37.03% |
| 1998 | 39.60% | $278,450 | $369,604 |     | $83,870 | $285,734 | 36.96% |
| 1999 | 39.60% | $283,150 | $369,162 |     | $85,289 | $283,873 | 36.92% |
| 2000 | 39.60% | $288,350 | $368,668 |     | $86,855 | $281,813 | 36.87% |
| 2001 | 39.10% | $297,350 | $363,043 |     | $88,307 | $274,736 | 36.30% |
| 2002 | 38.60% | $307,050 | $356,760 |     | $89,281 | $267,479 | 35.68% |
| 2003 | 35.00% | $311,950 | $325,207 |     | $84,389 | $240,818 | 32.52% |
| 2004 | 35.00% | $319,100 | $324,643 |     | $86,328 | $238,315 | 32.46% |
| 2005 | 35.00% | $326,450 | $324,063 |     | $88,320 | $235,743 | 32.41% |
| 2006 | 35.00% | $336,550 | $323,251 |     | $91,043 | $232,208 | 32.33% |
| 2007 | 35.00% | $349,700 | $322,206 |     | $94,601 | $227,605 | 32.22% |
| 2008 | 35.00% | $357,700 | $321,575 |     | $96,770 | $224,805 | 32.16% |
| 2009 | 35.00% | $372,950 | $320,363 |     | $100,895 | $219,468 | 32.04% |
| 2010 | 35.00% | $373,650 | $320,309 |     | $101,086 | $219,223 | 32.03% |
| 2011 | 35.00% | $379,150 | $319,872 |     | $102,574 | $217,298 | 31.99% |

See Appendix B 3.3 for notes

Notes to Appendices B-3.1 and B-3.2
Individual Income Tax and Effective Tax Rates
Taxable income of $1,000,000
1953-2011
(in current dollars)

Source: Tax Rates: Internal Revenue Service Instructions to Form 1040 and Tax Rate
Tables of respective years - Married, filing jointly

* Rate at which income is taxed above Top Bracket Amount

Surcharge 1968-1970

(1)   Includes 10% surcharge from April = 7.5% surcharge

(2)   Includes 10% surcharge thru June=5% plus 5% thru December

(3)   Includes 5%% surcharge thru June=2.5%

Credit 1981

(4)   Includes 1.25% credit against calculated tax

Tax calculation 1988 - 1990

|  |  | (5) 1988 |  | (6) 1989 |  | (7) 1990 |  |
|---|---|---|---|---|---|---|---|
| Base tax | 1 |  | $41,790 |  | $43,490 |  | $45,576 |
| Taxable income | 2 | $1,000,000 |  | $1,000,000 |  | $1,000,000 |  |
| Top tax bracket | 3 | $149,250 |  | $155,320 |  | $162,770 |  |
| Excess over top | 4 | $850,750 |  | $844,680 |  | $837,230 |  |
| Tax at 28% | 5 |  | $238,210 |  | $236,510 |  | $234,424 |
| Tax at 5% | 6 | $42,538 |  | $42,234 |  | $41,862 |  |
| Exemptions** | 7 | $1,092 |  | $1,120 |  | $1,148 |  |
| Lesser of 6 or 7 | 8 |  | $1,092 |  | $1,120 |  | $1,148 |
| Total tax | 9 |  | $281,092 |  | $281,120 |  | $281,148 |

| ** Exemptions | 2 | $546 | 2 | $560 | 2 | 574 |
|---|---|---|---|---|---|---|

## Individual Income Tax and Effective Tax Rates
### Taxable income of $400,000
### 1953-1982
### (in current dollars)

| Year | Top Bracket Rate * | Top Bracket Amount | Bracket at or Before $400,000 Rate** | Bracket at or Before $400,000 Amount | Tax at $400,000 Amount | | Base Tax | Excess | Effective Tax Rate |
|---|---|---|---|---|---|---|---|---|---|
| 1953 | 92.00% | $200,000 | 92.00% | $200,000 | $344,716 | | $160,716 | $184,000 | 86.2% |
| 1954 | 91.00% | $200,000 | 91.00% | $200,000 | $338,820 | | $156,820 | $182,000 | 84.7% |
| 1955 | 91.00% | $400,000 | 91.00% | $400,000 | $313,640 | | $313,640 | | 78.4% |
| 1956 | 91.00% | $400,000 | 91.00% | $400,000 | $313,640 | | $313,640 | | 78.4% |
| 1957 | 91.00% | $400,000 | 91.00% | $400,000 | $313,640 | | $313,640 | | 78.4% |
| 1958 | 91.00% | $400,000 | 91.00% | $400,000 | $313,640 | | $313,640 | | 78.4% |
| 1959 | 91.00% | $400,000 | 91.00% | $400,000 | $313,640 | | $313,640 | | 78.4% |
| 1960 | 91.00% | $400,000 | 91.00% | $400,000 | $313,640 | | $313,640 | | 78.4% |
| 1961 | 91.00% | $400,000 | 91.00% | $400,000 | $313,640 | | $313,640 | | 78.4% |
| 1962 | 91.00% | $400,000 | 91.00% | $400,000 | $313,640 | | $313,640 | | 78.4% |
| 1963 | 91.00% | $400,000 | 91.00% | $400,000 | $313,640 | | $313,640 | | 78.4% |
| 1964 | 77.00% | $400,000 | 77.00% | $400,000 | $271,680 | | $271,680 | | 67.9% |
| 1965 | 70.00% | $200,000 | 70.00% | $200,000 | $250,980 | | $110,980 | $140,000 | 62.7% |
| 1966 | 70.00% | $200,000 | 70.00% | $200,000 | $250,980 | | $110,980 | $140,000 | 62.7% |
| 1967 | 70.00% | $200,000 | 70.00% | $200,000 | $250,980 | | $110,980 | $140,000 | 62.7% |
| 1968 | 70.00% | $200,000 | 70.00% | $200,000 | $269,804 | (1) | $110,980 | $140,000 | 67.5% |
| 1969 | 70.00% | $200,000 | 70.00% | $200,000 | $276,078 | (2) | $110,980 | $140,000 | 69.0% |
| 1970 | 70.00% | $200,000 | 70.00% | $200,000 | $257,255 | (3) | $110,980 | $140,000 | 64.3% |
| 1971 | 70.00% | $200,000 | 70.00% | $200,000 | $250,980 | | $110,980 | $140,000 | 62.7% |
| 1972 | 70.00% | $200,000 | 70.00% | $200,000 | $250,980 | | $110,980 | $140,000 | 62.7% |
| 1973 | 70.00% | $200,000 | 70.00% | $200,000 | $250,980 | | $110,980 | $140,000 | 62.7% |
| 1974 | 70.00% | $200,000 | 70.00% | $200,000 | $250,980 | | $110,980 | $140,000 | 62.7% |
| 1975 | 70.00% | $200,000 | 70.00% | $200,000 | $250,980 | | $110,980 | $140,000 | 62.7% |
| 1976 | 70.00% | $200,000 | 70.00% | $200,000 | $250,980 | | $110,980 | $140,000 | 62.7% |
| 1977 | 70.00% | $203,200 | 70.00% | $202,300 | $248,740 | | $110,980 | $137,760 | 62.2% |
| 1978 | 70.00% | $203,200 | 70.00% | $202,300 | $248,740 | | $110,980 | $137,760 | 62.2% |
| 1979 | 70.00% | $215,400 | 70.00% | $215,400 | $246,724 | | $117,504 | $129,220 | 61.7% |
| 1980 | 70.00% | $215,400 | 70.00% | $215,400 | $246,724 | | $117,504 | $129,220 | 61.7% |
| 1981 | 70.00% | $215,400 | 70.00% | $215,400 | $243,640 | (4) | $117,504 | $129,220 | 60.9% |
| 1982 | 50.00% | $85,600 | 50.00% | $85,600 | $187,449 | | $30,249 | $157,200 | 46.9% |

See Appendix B 4.3 for notes

## Individual Income Tax and Effective Tax Rates
### Taxable income of $400,000
### 1982-2011
### (in current dollars)

| Year | Top Bracket | | Bracket at or Before $400,000 | | Tax at $400,000 | | Base Tax | Excess | Effective Tax Rate |
|------|---------|----------|----------|----------|-----------|-----|----------|----------|------|
| | Rate * | Amount | Rate** | Amount | Amount | | Tax | Excess | Rate |
| 1983 | 50.00% | $109,400 | 50.00% | $109,400 | $184,002 | | $38,702 | $145,300 | 46.0% |
| 1984 | 50.00% | $162,400 | 50.00% | $162,400 | $181,400 | | $62,600 | $118,800 | 45.4% |
| 1985 | 50.00% | $169,020 | 50.00% | $169,020 | $180,642 | | $65,152 | $115,490 | 45.2% |
| 1986 | 50.00% | $175,250 | 50.00% | $175,250 | $179,928 | | $67,553 | $112,375 | 45.0% |
| 1987 | 38.50% | $90,000 | 38.50% | $90,000 | $143,940 | | $24,590 | $119,350 | 36.0% |
| 1988 | 28.00% | $149,250 | 28.00% | $149,250 | $113,092 | (5) | | | 28.3% |
| 1989 | 28.00% | $155,320 | 28.00% | $155,320 | $113,120 | (6) | | | 28.3% |
| 1990 | 28.00% | $162,770 | 28.00% | $162,770 | $113,148 | (7) | | | 28.3% |
| 1991 | 31.00% | $82,150 | 31.00% | $82,150 | $117,116 | | $18,582 | $98,534 | 29.3% |
| 1992 | 31.00% | $86,500 | 31.00% | $86,500 | $116,751 | | $19,566 | $97,185 | 29.2% |
| 1993 | 39.60% | $250,000 | 39.60% | $250,000 | $134,929 | | $75,529 | $59,400 | 33.7% |
| 1994 | 39.60% | $250,000 | 39.60% | $250,000 | $134,705 | | $75,305 | $59,400 | 33.7% |
| 1995 | 39.60% | $256,500 | 39.60% | $143,600 | $134,089 | | $77,263 | $56,826 | 33.5% |
| 1996 | 39.60% | $263,750 | 39.60% | $147,700 | $133,400 | | $79,445 | $53,955 | 33.4% |
| 1997 | 39.60% | $271,050 | 39.60% | $151,750 | $132,711 | | $81,647 | $51,064 | 33.2% |
| 1998 | 39.60% | $278,450 | 39.60% | $155,950 | $132,004 | | $83,870 | $48,134 | 33.0% |
| 1999 | 39.60% | $283,150 | 39.60% | $158,550 | $131,562 | | $85,289 | $46,273 | 32.9% |
| 2000 | 39.60% | $288,350 | 39.60% | $161,450 | $131,068 | | $86,855 | $44,213 | 32.8% |
| 2001 | 39.10% | $297,350 | 39.10% | $166,500 | $128,443 | | $88,307 | $40,136 | 32.1% |
| 2002 | 38.60% | $307,050 | 38.60% | $171,950 | $125,160 | | $89,281 | $35,879 | 31.3% |
| 2003 | 35.00% | $311,950 | 35.00% | $174,700 | $115,207 | | $84,389 | $30,818 | 28.8% |
| 2004 | 35.00% | $319,100 | 35.00% | $178,650 | $114,643 | | $86,328 | $28,315 | 28.7% |
| 2005 | 35.00% | $326,450 | 35.00% | $182,800 | $114,063 | | $88,320 | $25,743 | 28.5% |
| 2006 | 35.00% | $336,550 | 35.00% | $188,450 | $113,251 | | $91,043 | $22,208 | 28.3% |
| 2007 | 35.00% | $349,700 | 35.00% | $195,850 | $112,206 | | $94,601 | $17,605 | 28.1% |
| 2008 | 35.00% | $357,700 | 35.00% | $200,300 | $111,575 | | $96,770 | $14,805 | 27.9% |
| 2009 | 35.00% | $372,950 | 35.00% | $208,850 | $110,363 | | $100,895 | $9,468 | 27.6% |
| 2010 | 35.00% | $373,650 | 35.00% | $209,250 | $110,309 | | $101,086 | $9,223 | 27.6% |
| 2011 | 35.00% | $379,150 | 35.00% | $212,300 | $109,872 | | $102,574 | $7,298 | 27.5% |

See Appendix B-4.3 for notes

Notes to Appendices B 4.1 and B 4.2
Individual Income Tax and Effective Tax Rates
Taxable income of $400,000
1953-2011
(in current dollars)

Source:  Tax Rates:  Internal Revenue Service Instructions to Form 1040 and Tax Rate
Tables of respective years - Married, filing jointly

 *  Rate at which income is taxed above Top Bracket Amount
** Rate at which $400,000 income is taxed

Surcharge 1968-1970

(1)   Includes 10% surcharge from April = 7.5% surcharge

(2)   Includes 10% surcharge thru June=5% plus 5% thru December

(3)   Includes 5%% surcharge thru June=2.5%

Credit 1981

(4)   Includes 1.25% credit against calculated tax

Tax calculation 1988 - 1990

|  |  | (4) 1988 |  | (5) 1989 |  | (6) 1990 |  |
|---|---|---|---|---|---|---|---|
| Base tax | 1 |  | $41,790 |  | $43,490 |  | $45,576 |
| Taxable income | 2 | $400,000 |  | $400,000 |  | $400,000 |  |
| Top tax bracket | 3 | $149,250 |  | $155,320 |  | $162,770 |  |
| Excess over top | 4 | $250,750 |  | $244,680 |  | $237,230 |  |
| Tax at 28% | 5 |  | $70,210 |  | $68,510 |  | $66,424 |
| Tax at 5% | 6 | $12,538 |  | $12,234 |  | $11,862 |  |
| Exemptions*** | 7 | $1,092 |  | $1,120 |  | $1,148 |  |
| Lesser of 6 or 7 | 8 |  | $1,092 |  | $1,120 |  | $1,148 |
| Total tax | 9 |  | $113,092 |  | $113,120 |  | $113,148 |

| *** Exemptions | 2 | $546 | 2 | $560 | 2 | 574 |
|---|---|---|---|---|---|---|

Individual Income Tax and Effective Tax Rates
Taxable income of $250,000
1953-1982
(in current dollars)

| Year | Top Bracket Rate * | Top Bracket Amount | Bracket at or Before $250,000 Rate** | Bracket at or Before $250,000 Amount | Tax at $250,000 Amount | | Base Tax | Excess | Effective Tax Rate |
|------|------|------|------|------|------|---|------|------|------|
| 1953 | 92.00% | $200,000 | 92.00% | $200,000 | $206,716 | | $160,716 | $46,000 | 82.69% |
| 1954 | 91.00% | $200,000 | 91.00% | $200,000 | $202,320 | | $156,820 | $45,500 | 80.93% |
| 1955 | 91.00% | $400,000 | 89.00% | $200,000 | $179,140 | | $134,640 | $44,500 | 71.66% |
| 1956 | 91.00% | $400,000 | 89.00% | $200,000 | $179,140 | | $134,640 | $44,500 | 71.66% |
| 1957 | 91.00% | $400,000 | 89.00% | $200,000 | $179,140 | | $134,640 | $44,500 | 71.66% |
| 1958 | 91.00% | $400,000 | 89.00% | $200,000 | $179,140 | | $134,640 | $44,500 | 71.66% |
| 1959 | 91.00% | $400,000 | 89.00% | $200,000 | $179,140 | | $134,640 | $44,500 | 71.66% |
| 1960 | 91.00% | $400,000 | 89.00% | $200,000 | $179,140 | | $134,640 | $44,500 | 71.66% |
| 1961 | 91.00% | $400,000 | 89.00% | $200,000 | $179,140 | | $134,640 | $44,500 | 71.66% |
| 1962 | 91.00% | $400,000 | 89.00% | $200,000 | $179,140 | | $134,640 | $44,500 | 71.66% |
| 1963 | 91.00% | $400,000 | 89.00% | $200,000 | $179,140 | | $134,640 | $44,500 | 71.66% |
| 1964 | 77.00% | $400,000 | 76.50% | $200,000 | $156,930 | | $118,680 | $38,250 | 62.77% |
| 1965 | 70.00% | $200,000 | 70.00% | $200,000 | $145,980 | | $110,980 | $35,000 | 58.39% |
| 1966 | 70.00% | $200,000 | 70.00% | $200,000 | $145,980 | | $110,980 | $35,000 | 58.39% |
| 1967 | 70.00% | $200,000 | 70.00% | $200,000 | $145,980 | | $110,980 | $35,000 | 58.39% |
| 1968 | 70.00% | $200,000 | 70.00% | $200,000 | $156,929 | (1) | $110,980 | $35,000 | 62.77% |
| 1969 | 70.00% | $200,000 | 70.00% | $200,000 | $160,578 | (2) | $110,980 | $35,000 | 64.23% |
| 1970 | 70.00% | $200,000 | 70.00% | $200,000 | $149,630 | (3) | $110,980 | $35,000 | 59.85% |
| 1971 | 70.00% | $200,000 | 70.00% | $200,000 | $145,980 | | $110,980 | $35,000 | 58.39% |
| 1972 | 70.00% | $200,000 | 70.00% | $200,000 | $145,980 | | $110,980 | $35,000 | 58.39% |
| 1973 | 70.00% | $200,000 | 70.00% | $200,000 | $145,980 | | $110,980 | $35,000 | 58.39% |
| 1974 | 70.00% | $200,000 | 70.00% | $200,000 | $145,980 | | $110,980 | $35,000 | 58.39% |
| 1975 | 70.00% | $200,000 | 70.00% | $200,000 | $145,980 | | $110,980 | $35,000 | 58.39% |
| 1976 | 70.00% | $200,000 | 70.00% | $200,000 | $145,980 | | $110,980 | $35,000 | 58.39% |
| 1977 | 70.00% | $203,200 | 70.00% | $202,300 | $144,370 | | $110,980 | $33,390 | 57.75% |
| 1978 | 70.00% | $203,200 | 70.00% | $202,300 | $144,370 | | $110,980 | $33,390 | 57.75% |
| 1979 | 70.00% | $215,400 | 70.00% | $215,400 | $141,724 | | $117,504 | $24,220 | 56.69% |
| 1980 | 70.00% | $215,400 | 70.00% | $215,400 | $141,724 | | $117,504 | $24,220 | 56.69% |
| 1981 | 70.00% | $215,400 | 70.00% | $215,400 | $139,952 | (4) | $117,504 | $24,220 | 55.98% |
| 1982 | 50.00% | $85,600 | 50.00% | $85,600 | $112,449 | | $30,249 | $82,200 | 44.98% |

See Appendix B 5.3 for notes

Individual Income Tax and Effective Tax Rates
Taxable income of $250,000
1983-2011
(in current dollars)

| Year | Top Bracket Rate* | Top Bracket Amount | Bracket at or Before $250,000 Rate** | Bracket at or Before $250,000 Amount | Tax at $250,000 Amount | Base Tax | Excess | Effective Tax Rate |
|---|---|---|---|---|---|---|---|---|
| 1983 | 50.00% | $109,400 | 50.00% | $109,400 | $109,002 | $38,702 | $70,300 | 43.60% |
| 1984 | 50.00% | $162,400 | 50.00% | $162,400 | $106,400 | $62,600 | $43,800 | 42.56% |
| 1985 | 50.00% | $169,020 | 50.00% | $169,020 | $105,642 | $65,152 | $40,490 | 42.26% |
| 1986 | 50.00% | $175,250 | 50.00% | $175,250 | $104,928 | $67,553 | $37,375 | 41.97% |
| 1987 | 38.50% | $90,000 | 38.50% | $90,000 | $86,190 | $24,590 | $61,600 | 34.48% |
| 1988 | 28.00% | $149,250 | 28.00% | $149,250 | $71,092 (5) | | | 28.54% |
| 1989 | 28.00% | $155,320 | 28.00% | $155,320 | $71,120 (6) | | | 28.55% |
| 1990 | 28.00% | $162,770 | 28.00% | $162,770 | $71,148 (7) | | | 28.46% |
| 1991 | 31.00% | $82,150 | 31.00% | $82,150 | $70,616 | $18,582 | $52,034 | 28.25% |
| 1992 | 31.00% | $86,500 | 31.00% | $86,500 | $70,251 | $19,566 | $50,685 | 28.10% |
| 1993 | 39.60% | $250,000 | 36.00% | $250,000 | $75,529 | $75,529 | | 30.21% |
| 1994 | 39.60% | $250,000 | 36.00% | $250,000 | $75,305 | $75,305 | | 30.12% |
| 1995 | 39.60% | $256,500 | 36.00% | $143,600 | $74,923 | $36,619 | $38,304 | 29.97% |
| 1996 | 39.60% | $263,750 | 36.00% | $147,700 | $74,495 | $37,667 | $36,828 | 29.80% |
| 1997 | 39.60% | $271,050 | 36.00% | $151,750 | $74,069 | $38,699 | $35,370 | 29.63% |
| 1998 | 39.60% | $278,450 | 36.00% | $155,950 | $73,628 | $39,770 | $33,858 | 29.45% |
| 1999 | 39.60% | $283,150 | 36.00% | $158,550 | $73,355 | $40,433 | $32,922 | 29.34% |
| 2000 | 39.60% | $288,350 | 36.00% | $161,450 | $73,049 | $41,171 | $31,878 | 29.22% |
| 2001 | 39.10% | $297,350 | 35.50% | $166,500 | $71,498 | $41,855 | $29,643 | 28.60% |
| 2002 | 38.60% | $307,050 | 35.00% | $171,950 | $69,314 | $41,996 | $27,318 | 27.73% |
| 2003 | 35.00% | $311,950 | 33.00% | $174,700 | $63,946 | $39,097 | $24,849 | 25.58% |
| 2004 | 35.00% | $319,100 | 33.00% | $178,650 | $63,526 | $39,980 | $23,546 | 25.41% |
| 2005 | 35.00% | $326,450 | 33.00% | $182,800 | $63,092 | $40,916 | $22,176 | 25.24% |
| 2006 | 35.00% | $336,550 | 33.00% | $188,450 | $62,482 | $42,170 | $20,312 | 24.99% |
| 2007 | 35.00% | $349,700 | 33.00% | $195,850 | $61,701 | $43,831 | $17,870 | 24.68% |
| 2008 | 35.00% | $357,700 | 33.00% | $200,300 | $61,229 | $44,828 | $16,401 | 24.49% |
| 2009 | 35.00% | $372,950 | 33.00% | $208,850 | $60,322 | $46,742 | $13,580 | 24.13% |
| 2010 | 35.00% | $373,650 | 33.00% | $209,250 | $60,282 | $46,834 | $13,448 | 24.11% |
| 2011 | 35.00% | $379,150 | 33.00% | $212,300 | $59,955 | $47,514 | $12,441 | 23.98% |

See Appendix B 5.3 for notes

Notes to Appendices B 5.1 and B 5.2
Individual Income Tax and Effective Tax Rates
Taxable income of $250,000
1953-2011
(in current dollars)


Source:  Tax Rates:  Internal Revenue Service Instructions to Form 1040 and Tax Rate
Tables of respective years - Married, filing jointly


 * Rate at which income is taxed above Top Bracket Amount
** Rate at which $250,000 income is taxed


Surcharge 1968-1970

(1)    Includes 10% surcharge from April = 7.5% surcharge

(2)    Includes 10% surcharge thru June=5% plus 5% thru December

(3)    Includes 5%% surcharge thru June=2.5%


Credit 1981

(4)    Includes 1.25% credit against calculated tax


Tax calculation 1988 - 1990

|  |  | (4) 1988 |  | (5) 1989 |  | (6) 1990 |  |
|---|---|---|---|---|---|---|---|
| Base tax | 1 |  | $41,790 |  | $43,490 |  | $45,576 |
| Taxable income | 2 | $250,000 |  | $250,000 |  | $250,000 |  |
| Top tax bracket | 3 | $149,250 |  | $155,320 |  | $162,770 |  |
| Excess over top | 4 | $100,750 |  | $94,680 |  | $87,230 |  |
| Tax at 28% | 5 |  | $28,210 |  | $26,510 |  | $24,424 |
| Tax at 5% | 6 | $5,038 |  | $4,734 |  | $4,362 |  |
| Exemptions*** | 7 | $1,092 |  | $1,120 |  | $1,148 |  |
| Lesser of 6 or 7 | 8 |  | $1,092 |  | $1,120 |  | $1,148 |
| Total tax | 9 |  | $71,092 |  | $71,120 |  | $71,148 |

| *** Exemptions | 2 | $546 | 2 | $560 | 2 | $574 |
|---|---|---|---|---|---|---|

## Individual Income Tax and Effective Tax Rates
### Taxable income of $200,000
### 1953-1982
### (in current dollars)

| Year | Top Bracket | | Bracket at or Before $200,000 | | Tax at $200,000 | | Base Tax | Excess | Effective Tax Rate |
|------|-------------|--------|-------------|--------|-------------|-----|----------|--------|--------|
| | Rate * | Amount | Rate** | Amount | Amount | | | | |
| 1953 | 92.00% | $200,000 | 91.00% | $200,000 | $160,716 | | | | 80.4% |
| 1954 | 91.00% | $200,000 | 90.00% | $200,000 | $156,820 | | | | 78.4% |
| 1955 | 91.00% | $400,000 | 87.00% | $200,000 | $134,640 | | | | 67.3% |
| 1956 | 91.00% | $400,000 | 87.00% | $200,000 | $134,640 | | | | 67.3% |
| 1957 | 91.00% | $400,000 | 87.00% | $200,000 | $134,640 | | | | 67.3% |
| 1958 | 91.00% | $400,000 | 87.00% | $200,000 | $134,640 | | | | 67.3% |
| 1959 | 91.00% | $400,000 | 87.00% | $200,000 | $134,640 | | | | 67.3% |
| 1960 | 91.00% | $400,000 | 87.00% | $200,000 | $134,640 | | | | 67.3% |
| 1961 | 91.00% | $400,000 | 87.00% | $200,000 | $134,640 | | | | 67.3% |
| 1962 | 91.00% | $400,000 | 87.00% | $200,000 | $134,640 | | | | 67.3% |
| 1963 | 91.00% | $400,000 | 87.00% | $200,000 | $134,640 | | | | 67.3% |
| 1964 | 77.00% | $400,000 | 75.00% | $200,000 | $118,680 | | | | 59.3% |
| 1965 | 70.00% | $200,000 | 69.00% | $200,000 | $110,980 | | | | 55.5% |
| 1966 | 70.00% | $200,000 | 69.00% | $200,000 | $110,980 | | | | 55.5% |
| 1967 | 70.00% | $200,000 | 69.00% | $200,000 | $110,980 | | | | 55.5% |
| 1968 | 70.00% | $200,000 | 69.00% | $200,000 | $119,304 | (1) | $110,980 | $0 | 59.7% |
| 1969 | 70.00% | $200,000 | 69.00% | $200,000 | $122,078 | (2) | $110,980 | $0 | 61.0% |
| 1970 | 70.00% | $200,000 | 69.00% | $200,000 | $113,755 | (3) | $110,980 | $0 | 56.9% |
| 1971 | 70.00% | $200,000 | 69.00% | $200,000 | $110,980 | | | | 55.5% |
| 1972 | 70.00% | $200,000 | 69.00% | $200,000 | $110,980 | | | | 55.5% |
| 1973 | 70.00% | $200,000 | 69.00% | $200,000 | $110,980 | | | | 55.5% |
| 1974 | 70.00% | $200,000 | 69.00% | $200,000 | $110,980 | | | | 55.5% |
| 1975 | 70.00% | $200,000 | 69.00% | $200,000 | $110,980 | | | | 55.5% |
| 1976 | 70.00% | $200,000 | 69.00% | $200,000 | $110,980 | | | | 55.5% |
| 1977 | 70.00% | $203,200 | 69.00% | $183,200 | $108,772 | | $97,180 | $11,592 | 54.4% |
| 1978 | 70.00% | $203,200 | 69.00% | $183,200 | $108,772 | | $97,180 | $11,592 | 54.4% |
| 1979 | 70.00% | $215,400 | 68.00% | $162,400 | $107,032 | | $81,464 | $25,568 | 53.5% |
| 1980 | 70.00% | $215,400 | 68.00% | $162,400 | $107,032 | | $81,464 | $25,568 | 53.5% |
| 1981 | 70.00% | $215,400 | 68.00% | $162,400 | $105,694 | (4) | $81,464 | $25,568 | 52.8% |
| 1982 | 50.00% | $85,600 | 50.00% | $85,600 | $87,449 | | $30,249 | $57,200 | 43.7% |

See Appendix B 6.3 for notes

Individual Income Tax and Effective Tax Rates
Taxable income of $200,000
1983-2011
(in current dollars)

| Year | Top Bracket | | Bracket at or Before $200,000 | | Tax at $200,000 | | Base Tax | Excess | Effective Tax Rate |
|------|------|------|------|------|------|------|------|------|------|
| | Rate * | Amount | Rate** | Amount | Amount | | Tax | | |
| 1983 | 50.00% | $109,400 | 50.00% | $109,400 | $84,002 | | $38,702 | $45,300 | 42.0% |
| 1984 | 50.00% | $162,400 | 50.00% | $162,400 | $81,400 | | $62,600 | $18,800 | 40.7% |
| 1985 | 50.00% | $169,020 | 50.00% | $169,020 | $80,642 | | $65,152 | $15,490 | 40.3% |
| 1986 | 50.00% | $175,250 | 50.00% | $175,250 | $79,928 | | $67,553 | $12,375 | 40.0% |
| 1987 | 38.50% | $90,000 | 38.50% | $90,000 | $66,940 | | $24,590 | $42,350 | 33.5% |
| 1988 | 28.00% | $149,250 | 28.00% | $149,250 | $57,092 | (5) | | | 28.5% |
| 1989 | 28.00% | $155,320 | 28.00% | $155,320 | $57,120 | (6) | | | 28.6% |
| 1990 | 28.00% | $162,770 | 28.00% | $162,770 | $57,148 | (7) | | | 28.6% |
| 1991 | 31.00% | $82,150 | 31.00% | $82,150 | $55,116 | | $18,582 | $36,534 | 27.6% |
| 1992 | 31.00% | $86,500 | 31.00% | $86,500 | $54,751 | | $19,566 | $35,185 | 27.4% |
| 1993 | 39.60% | $250,000 | 36.00% | $140,000 | $57,529 | | $35,929 | $21,600 | 28.8% |
| 1994 | 39.60% | $250,000 | 36.00% | $140,000 | $57,305 | | $35,705 | $21,600 | 28.7% |
| 1995 | 39.60% | $256,500 | 36.00% | $143,600 | $56,923 | | $36,619 | $20,304 | 28.5% |
| 1996 | 39.60% | $263,750 | 36.00% | $147,700 | $56,495 | | $37,667 | $18,828 | 28.2% |
| 1997 | 39.60% | $271,050 | 36.00% | $151,750 | $56,069 | | $38,699 | $17,370 | 28.0% |
| 1998 | 39.60% | $278,450 | 36.00% | $155,950 | $55,628 | | $39,770 | $15,858 | 27.8% |
| 1999 | 39.60% | $283,150 | 36.00% | $158,550 | $55,355 | | $40,433 | $14,922 | 27.7% |
| 2000 | 39.60% | $288,350 | 36.00% | $161,450 | $55,049 | | $41,171 | $13,878 | 27.5% |
| 2001 | 39.10% | $297,350 | 35.50% | $166,500 | $53,748 | | $41,855 | $11,893 | 26.9% |
| 2002 | 38.60% | $307,050 | 35.00% | $171,950 | $51,814 | | $41,996 | $9,818 | 25.9% |
| 2003 | 35.00% | $311,950 | 33.00% | $174,700 | $47,446 | | $39,097 | $8,349 | 23.7% |
| 2004 | 35.00% | $319,100 | 33.00% | $178,650 | $47,026 | | $39,980 | $7,046 | 23.5% |
| 2005 | 35.00% | $326,450 | 33.00% | $182,800 | $46,592 | | $40,916 | $5,676 | 23.3% |
| 2006 | 35.00% | $336,550 | 33.00% | $188,450 | $45,982 | | $42,170 | $3,812 | 23.0% |
| 2007 | 35.00% | $349,700 | 33.00% | $195,850 | $45,201 | | $43,831 | $1,370 | 22.6% |
| 2008 | 35.00% | $357,700 | 28.00% | $131,450 | $44,744 | | $25,550 | $19,194 | 22.4% |
| 2009 | 35.00% | $372,950 | 28.00% | $137,050 | $44,264 | | $26,638 | $17,626 | 22.1% |
| 2010 | 35.00% | $373,650 | 28.00% | $137,300 | $44,244 | | $26,688 | $17,556 | 22.1% |
| 2011 | 35.00% | $379,150 | 28.00% | $139,350 | $44,070 | | $27,088 | $16,982 | 22.0% |

See Appendix B 6.3 for notes

Notes to Appendices B 6.1 and B 6.2
Individual Income Tax and Effective Tax Rates
Taxable income of $200,000
1953-2011
(in current dollars)


Source: Tax Rates: Internal Revenue Service Instructions to Form 1040 and Tax Rate
Tables of respective years - Married, filing jointly

 * Rate at which income is taxed above Top Bracket Amount
** Rate at which $200,000 income is taxed

Surcharge 1968-1970

      (1)   Includes 10% surcharge from April = 7.5% surcharge

      (2)   Includes 10% surcharge thru June=5% plus 5% thru December

      (3)   Includes 5%% surcharge thru June=2.5%

Credit 1981

      (4)   Includes 1.25% credit against calculated tax


|  |  | 1988 (4) |  | 1989 (5) |  | 1990 (6) |  |
|---|---|---|---|---|---|---|---|
| Base tax | 1 |  | $41,790 |  | $43,490 |  | $45,576 |
| Taxable income | 2 | 200,000 |  | 200,000 |  | 200,000 |  |
| Top tax bracket | 3 | 149,250 |  | 155,320 |  | 162,770 |  |
| Excess over top | 4 | 50,750 |  | 44,680 |  | 37,230 |  |
| Tax at 28% | 5 |  | 14,210 |  | 12,510 |  | 10,424 |
| Tax at 5% | 6 | 2,538 |  | 2,234 |  | 1,862 |  |
| Exemptions*** | 7 | 1,092 |  | 1,120 |  | 1,148 |  |
| Lesser of 6 or 7 | 8 |  | 1,092 |  | 1,120 |  | 1,148 |
| Total tax | 9 |  | $57,092 |  | $57,120 |  | $57,148 |
|  |  |  |  |  |  |  |  |
| *** Exemptions |  | 2 | $546 | 2 | $560 | 2 | $574 |

## Maximum Tax Rates and Changes in Maximum Tax Rates
### Varying Taxable Incomes
### 1953 - 1982

| Year | Maximum Rate | | | | Change in Maximum Rate | | | |
|------|-------------|-----------|-----------|-----------|-------------|-----------|-----------|-----------|
|      | $1,000,000 | $400,000 | $250,000 | $200,000 | $1,000,000 | $400,000 | $250,000 | $200,000 |
| 1953 | 92.00% | 92.00% | 92.00% | 91.00% | 0.00% | 0.00% | 0.00% | 0.00% |
| 1954 | 91.00% | 91.00% | 91.00% | 90.00% | -1.00% | -1.00% | -1.00% | -1.00% |
| 1955 | 91.00% | 91.00% | 89.00% | 87.00% | 0.00% | 0.00% | -2.00% | -3.00% |
| 1956 | 91.00% | 91.00% | 89.00% | 87.00% | 0.00% | 0.00% | 0.00% | 0.00% |
| 1957 | 91.00% | 91.00% | 89.00% | 87.00% | 0.00% | 0.00% | 0.00% | 0.00% |
| 1958 | 91.00% | 91.00% | 89.00% | 87.00% | 0.00% | 0.00% | 0.00% | 0.00% |
| 1959 | 91.00% | 91.00% | 89.00% | 87.00% | 0.00% | 0.00% | 0.00% | 0.00% |
| 1960 | 91.00% | 91.00% | 89.00% | 87.00% | 0.00% | 0.00% | 0.00% | 0.00% |
| 1961 | 91.00% | 91.00% | 89.00% | 87.00% | 0.00% | 0.00% | 0.00% | 0.00% |
| 1962 | 91.00% | 91.00% | 89.00% | 87.00% | 0.00% | 0.00% | 0.00% | 0.00% |
| 1963 | 91.00% | 91.00% | 89.00% | 87.00% | 0.00% | 0.00% | 0.00% | 0.00% |
| 1964 | 77.00% | 77.00% | 76.50% | 75.00% | -14.00% | -14.00% | -12.50% | -12.00% |
| 1965 | 70.00% | 70.00% | 70.00% | 69.00% | -7.00% | -7.00% | -6.50% | -6.00% |
| 1966 | 70.00% | 70.00% | 70.00% | 69.00% | 0.00% | 0.00% | 0.00% | 0.00% |
| 1967 | 70.00% | 70.00% | 70.00% | 69.00% | 0.00% | 0.00% | 0.00% | 0.00% |
| 1968 | 70.00% | 70.00% | 70.00% | 69.00% | 0.00% | 0.00% | 0.00% | 0.00% |
| 1969 | 70.00% | 70.00% | 70.00% | 69.00% | 0.00% | 0.00% | 0.00% | 0.00% |
| 1970 | 70.00% | 70.00% | 70.00% | 69.00% | 0.00% | 0.00% | 0.00% | 0.00% |
| 1971 | 70.00% | 70.00% | 70.00% | 69.00% | 0.00% | 0.00% | 0.00% | 0.00% |
| 1972 | 70.00% | 70.00% | 70.00% | 69.00% | 0.00% | 0.00% | 0.00% | 0.00% |
| 1973 | 70.00% | 70.00% | 70.00% | 69.00% | 0.00% | 0.00% | 0.00% | 0.00% |
| 1974 | 70.00% | 70.00% | 70.00% | 69.00% | 0.00% | 0.00% | 0.00% | 0.00% |
| 1975 | 70.00% | 70.00% | 70.00% | 69.00% | 0.00% | 0.00% | 0.00% | 0.00% |
| 1976 | 70.00% | 70.00% | 70.00% | 69.00% | 0.00% | 0.00% | 0.00% | 0.00% |
| 1977 | 70.00% | 70.00% | 70.00% | 69.00% | 0.00% | 0.00% | 0.00% | 0.00% |
| 1978 | 70.00% | 70.00% | 70.00% | 69.00% | 0.00% | 0.00% | 0.00% | 0.00% |
| 1979 | 70.00% | 70.00% | 70.00% | 68.00% | 0.00% | 0.00% | 0.00% | -1.00% |
| 1980 | 70.00% | 70.00% | 70.00% | 68.00% | 0.00% | 0.00% | 0.00% | 0.00% |
| 1981 | 70.00% | 70.00% | 70.00% | 68.00% | 0.00% | 0.00% | 0.00% | 0.00% |
| 1982 | 50.00% | 50.00% | 50.00% | 50.00% | -20.00% | -20.00% | -20.00% | -18.00% |

See Appendices B 3.3, B 4.3, B 5.3 and B 6.3 for notes

## Maximum Tax Rates and Changes in Maximum Tax Rates

### Varying Taxable Incomes

### 1983 - 2011

| Year | Maximum Rate | | | | Change in Maximum Rate | | | |
|------|-------------|-------------|-------------|-------------|-------------|-------------|-------------|-------------|
|      | $1,000,000 | $400,000 | $250,000 | $200,000 | $1,000,000 | $400,000 | $250,000 | $200,000 |
| 1983 | 50.00% | 50.00% | 50.00% | 50.00% | 0.00% | 0.00% | 0.00% | 0.00% |
| 1984 | 50.00% | 50.00% | 50.00% | 50.00% | 0.00% | 0.00% | 0.00% | 0.00% |
| 1985 | 50.00% | 50.00% | 50.00% | 50.00% | 0.00% | 0.00% | 0.00% | 0.00% |
| 1986 | 50.00% | 50.00% | 50.00% | 50.00% | 0.00% | 0.00% | 0.00% | 0.00% |
| 1987 | 38.50% | 38.50% | 38.50% | 38.50% | -11.50% | -11.50% | -11.50% | -11.50% |
| 1988 | 28.00% | 28.00% | 28.00% | 28.00% | -10.50% | -10.50% | -10.50% | -10.50% |
| 1989 | 28.00% | 28.00% | 28.00% | 28.00% | 0.00% | 0.00% | 0.00% | 0.00% |
| 1990 | 28.00% | 28.00% | 28.00% | 28.00% | 0.00% | 0.00% | 0.00% | 0.00% |
| 1991 | 31.00% | 31.00% | 31.00% | 31.00% | 3.00% | 3.00% | 3.00% | 3.00% |
| 1992 | 31.00% | 31.00% | 31.00% | 31.00% | 0.00% | 0.00% | 0.00% | 0.00% |
| 1993 | 39.60% | 39.60% | 36.00% | 36.00% | 8.60% | 8.60% | 5.00% | 5.00% |
| 1994 | 39.60% | 39.60% | 36.00% | 36.00% | 0.00% | 0.00% | 0.00% | 0.00% |
| 1995 | 39.60% | 39.60% | 36.00% | 36.00% | 0.00% | 0.00% | 0.00% | 0.00% |
| 1996 | 39.60% | 39.60% | 36.00% | 36.00% | 0.00% | 0.00% | 0.00% | 0.00% |
| 1997 | 39.60% | 39.60% | 36.00% | 36.00% | 0.00% | 0.00% | 0.00% | 0.00% |
| 1998 | 39.60% | 39.60% | 36.00% | 36.00% | 0.00% | 0.00% | 0.00% | 0.00% |
| 1999 | 39.60% | 39.60% | 36.00% | 36.00% | 0.00% | 0.00% | 0.00% | 0.00% |
| 2000 | 39.60% | 39.60% | 36.00% | 36.00% | 0.00% | 0.00% | 0.00% | 0.00% |
| 2001 | 39.10% | 39.10% | 35.50% | 35.50% | -0.50% | -0.50% | -0.50% | -0.50% |
| 2002 | 38.60% | 38.60% | 35.00% | 35.00% | -0.50% | -0.50% | -0.50% | -0.50% |
| 2003 | 35.00% | 35.00% | 33.00% | 33.00% | -3.60% | -3.60% | -2.00% | -2.00% |
| 2004 | 35.00% | 35.00% | 33.00% | 33.00% | 0.00% | 0.00% | 0.00% | 0.00% |
| 2005 | 35.00% | 35.00% | 33.00% | 33.00% | 0.00% | 0.00% | 0.00% | 0.00% |
| 2006 | 35.00% | 35.00% | 33.00% | 33.00% | 0.00% | 0.00% | 0.00% | 0.00% |
| 2007 | 35.00% | 35.00% | 33.00% | 33.00% | 0.00% | 0.00% | 0.00% | 0.00% |
| 2008 | 35.00% | 35.00% | 33.00% | 28.00% | 0.00% | 0.00% | 0.00% | -5.00% |
| 2009 | 35.00% | 35.00% | 33.00% | 28.00% | 0.00% | 0.00% | 0.00% | 0.00% |
| 2010 | 35.00% | 35.00% | 33.00% | 28.00% | 0.00% | 0.00% | 0.00% | 0.00% |
| 2011 | 35.00% | 35.00% | 33.00% | 28.00% | 0.00% | 0.00% | 0.00% | 0.00% |

See Appendices B 3.3, B 4.3, B 5.3 and B 6.3 for notes

## Effective Income Tax Rates and Changes in Effective Income Tax Rates
### Varying Taxable Incomes
### 1953 - 1982

| Year | Effective Tax Rate | | | | Change in Effective Tax Rate | | | |
|------|-------------|-----------|-----------|-----------|-------------|-----------|-----------|-----------|
| | $1,000,000 | $400,000 | $250,000 | $200,000 | $1,000,000 | $400,000 | $250,000 | $200,000 |
| 1953 | 89.7% | 86.18% | 82.69% | 80.36% | 0.00% | 0.00% | 0.00% | 0.00% |
| 1954 | 88.5% | 84.71% | 80.93% | 78.41% | -1.19% | -1.47% | -1.76% | -1.95% |
| 1955 | 86.0% | 78.41% | 71.66% | 67.32% | -2.52% | -6.30% | -9.27% | -11.09% |
| 1956 | 86.0% | 78.41% | 71.66% | 67.32% | 0.00% | 0.00% | 0.00% | 0.00% |
| 1957 | 86.0% | 78.41% | 71.66% | 67.32% | 0.00% | 0.00% | 0.00% | 0.00% |
| 1958 | 86.0% | 78.41% | 71.66% | 67.32% | 0.00% | 0.00% | 0.00% | 0.00% |
| 1959 | 86.0% | 78.41% | 71.66% | 67.32% | 0.00% | 0.00% | 0.00% | 0.00% |
| 1960 | 86.0% | 78.41% | 71.66% | 67.32% | 0.00% | 0.00% | 0.00% | 0.00% |
| 1961 | 86.0% | 78.41% | 71.66% | 67.32% | 0.00% | 0.00% | 0.00% | 0.00% |
| 1962 | 86.0% | 78.41% | 71.66% | 67.32% | 0.00% | 0.00% | 0.00% | 0.00% |
| 1963 | 86.0% | 78.41% | 71.66% | 67.32% | 0.00% | 0.00% | 0.00% | 0.00% |
| 1964 | 73.4% | 67.92% | 62.77% | 59.34% | -12.60% | -10.49% | -8.88% | -7.98% |
| 1965 | 67.1% | 62.75% | 58.39% | 55.49% | -6.27% | -5.18% | -4.38% | -3.85% |
| 1966 | 67.1% | 62.75% | 58.39% | 55.49% | 0.00% | 0.00% | 0.00% | 0.00% |
| 1967 | 67.1% | 62.75% | 58.39% | 55.49% | 0.00% | 0.00% | 0.00% | 0.00% |
| 1968 | 72.1% | 67.45% | 62.77% | 59.65% | 5.03% | 4.71% | 4.38% | 4.16% |
| 1969 | 73.8% | 69.02% | 64.23% | 61.04% | 1.68% | 1.57% | 1.46% | 1.39% |
| 1970 | 68.8% | 64.31% | 59.85% | 56.88% | -5.03% | -4.71% | -4.38% | -4.16% |
| 1971 | 67.1% | 62.75% | 58.39% | 55.49% | -1.68% | -1.57% | -1.46% | -1.39% |
| 1972 | 67.1% | 62.75% | 58.39% | 55.49% | 0.00% | 0.00% | 0.00% | 0.00% |
| 1973 | 67.1% | 62.75% | 58.39% | 55.49% | 0.00% | 0.00% | 0.00% | 0.00% |
| 1974 | 67.1% | 62.75% | 58.39% | 55.49% | 0.00% | 0.00% | 0.00% | 0.00% |
| 1975 | 67.1% | 62.75% | 58.39% | 55.49% | 0.00% | 0.00% | 0.00% | 0.00% |
| 1976 | 67.1% | 62.75% | 58.39% | 55.49% | 0.00% | 0.00% | 0.00% | 0.00% |
| 1977 | 66.9% | 62.19% | 57.75% | 54.39% | -0.22% | -0.56% | -0.64% | -1.10% |
| 1978 | 66.9% | 62.19% | 57.75% | 54.39% | 0.00% | 0.00% | 0.00% | 0.00% |
| 1979 | 66.7% | 61.68% | 56.69% | 53.52% | -0.20% | -0.50% | -1.06% | -0.87% |
| 1980 | 66.7% | 61.68% | 56.69% | 53.52% | 0.00% | 0.00% | 0.00% | 0.00% |
| 1981 | 65.8% | 60.91% | 55.98% | 52.85% | -0.83% | -0.77% | -0.71% | -0.67% |
| 1982 | 48.7% | 46.86% | 44.98% | 43.72% | -17.09% | -14.05% | -11.00% | -9.12% |

See Appendices B 3.3, B 4.3, B 5.3 and B 6.3 for notes

## Effective Income Tax Rates and Changes in Effective Income Tax Rates
## Varying Taxable Incomes
### 1983 - 2011

| Year | Effective Tax Rate | | | | Change in Effective Tax Rate | | | |
|---|---|---|---|---|---|---|---|---|
| | $1,000,000 | $400,000 | $250,000 | $200,000 | $1,000,000 | $400,000 | $250,000 | $200,000 |
| 1983 | 48.4% | 46.00% | 43.60% | 42.00% | 0.00% | 0.00% | 0.00% | 0.00% |
| 1984 | 48.1% | 45.35% | 42.56% | 40.70% | -0.26% | -0.65% | -1.04% | -1.30% |
| 1985 | 48.1% | 45.16% | 42.26% | 40.32% | -0.08% | -0.19% | -0.30% | -0.38% |
| 1986 | 48.0% | 44.98% | 41.97% | 39.96% | -0.07% | -0.18% | -0.29% | -0.36% |
| 1987 | 37.5% | 35.99% | 34.48% | 33.47% | -10.50% | -9.00% | -7.50% | -6.49% |
| 1988 | 28.1% | 28.27% | 28.54% | 28.55% | -9.38% | -7.71% | -5.94% | -4.92% |
| 1989 | 28.1% | 28.28% | 28.55% | 28.56% | 0.00% | 0.01% | 0.01% | 0.01% |
| 1990 | 28.1% | 28.29% | 28.46% | 28.57% | 0.00% | 0.01% | -0.09% | 0.01% |
| 1991 | 30.3% | 29.28% | 28.25% | 27.56% | 2.20% | 0.99% | -0.21% | -1.02% |
| 1992 | 30.3% | 29.19% | 28.10% | 27.38% | -0.04% | -0.09% | -0.15% | -0.18% |
| 1993 | 37.3% | 33.73% | 30.21% | 28.76% | 6.98% | 4.54% | 2.11% | 1.39% |
| 1994 | 37.2% | 33.68% | 30.12% | 28.65% | -0.02% | -0.06% | -0.09% | -0.11% |
| 1995 | 37.2% | 33.52% | 29.97% | 28.46% | -0.06% | -0.15% | -0.15% | -0.19% |
| 1996 | 37.1% | 33.35% | 29.80% | 28.25% | -0.07% | -0.17% | -0.17% | -0.21% |
| 1997 | 37.0% | 33.18% | 29.63% | 28.03% | -0.07% | -0.17% | -0.17% | -0.21% |
| 1998 | 37.0% | 33.00% | 29.45% | 27.81% | -0.07% | -0.18% | -0.18% | -0.22% |
| 1999 | 36.9% | 32.89% | 29.34% | 27.68% | -0.04% | -0.11% | -0.11% | -0.14% |
| 2000 | 36.9% | 32.77% | 29.22% | 27.52% | -0.05% | -0.12% | -0.12% | -0.15% |
| 2001 | 36.3% | 32.11% | 28.60% | 26.87% | -0.56% | -0.66% | -0.62% | -0.65% |
| 2002 | 35.7% | 31.29% | 27.73% | 25.91% | -0.63% | -0.82% | -0.87% | -0.97% |
| 2003 | 32.5% | 28.80% | 25.58% | 23.72% | -3.16% | -2.49% | -2.15% | -2.18% |
| 2004 | 32.5% | 28.66% | 25.41% | 23.51% | -0.06% | -0.14% | -0.17% | -0.21% |
| 2005 | 32.4% | 28.52% | 25.24% | 23.30% | -0.06% | -0.15% | -0.17% | -0.22% |
| 2006 | 32.3% | 28.31% | 24.99% | 22.99% | -0.08% | -0.20% | -0.24% | -0.31% |
| 2007 | 32.2% | 28.05% | 24.68% | 22.60% | -0.10% | -0.26% | -0.31% | -0.39% |
| 2008 | 32.2% | 27.89% | 24.49% | 22.37% | -0.06% | -0.16% | -0.19% | -0.23% |
| 2009 | 32.0% | 27.59% | 24.13% | 22.13% | -0.12% | -0.30% | -0.36% | -0.24% |
| 2010 | 32.0% | 27.58% | 24.11% | 22.12% | -0.01% | -0.01% | -0.02% | -0.01% |
| 2011 | 32.0% | 27.47% | 23.98% | 22.04% | -0.04% | -0.11% | -0.13% | -0.09% |

See Appendices B 3.3, B 4.3, B 5.3 and B 6.3 for notes

Individual Income Taxes
Capital Gains Tax Rates
1953-2011

| Year | Capital Gains Tax Rate | Year | Capital Gains Tax Rate |
|------|------------------------|------|------------------------|
| 1953 | 25.00% | 1983 | 20.00% |
| 1954 | 25.00% | 1984 | 20.00% |
| 1955 | 25.00% | 1985 | 20.00% |
| 1956 | 25.00% | 1986 | 20.00% |
| 1957 | 25.00% | 1987 | 28.00% |
| 1958 | 25.00% | 1988 | 33.00% |
| 1959 | 25.00% | 1989 | 33.00% |
| 1960 | 25.00% | 1990 | 28.00% |
| 1961 | 25.00% | 1991 | 28.00% |
| 1962 | 25.00% | 1992 | 28.00% |
| 1963 | 25.00% | 1993 | 28.00% |
| 1964 | 25.00% | 1994 | 28.00% |
| 1965 | 25.00% | 1995 | 28.00% |
| 1966 | 25.00% | 1996 | 28.00% |
| 1967 | 25.00% | 1997 | 28.00% |
| 1968 | 26.90% | 1998 | 28.00% |
| 1969 | 27.50% | 1999 | 28.00% |
| 1970 | 32.30% | 2000 | 20.00% |
| 1971 | 34.30% | 2001 | 20.00% |
| 1972 | 36.50% | 2002 | 20.00% |
| 1973 | 36.50% | 2003 | 15.00% |
| 1974 | 36.50% | 2004 | 15.00% |
| 1975 | 36.50% | 2005 | 15.00% |
| 1976 | 39.90% | 2006 | 15.00% |
| 1977 | 39.90% | 2007 | 15.00% |
| 1978 | 39.00% | 2008 | 15.00% |
| 1979 | 28.00% | 2009 | 15.00% |
| 1980 | 28.00% | 2010 | 15.00% |
| 1981 | 23.70% | 2011 | 15.00% |
| 1982 | 20.00% | | |

Source: Citizens for Tax Justice, November 2011.

## Corporate Income Taxes
## Top Marginal Rates
## 1953-2011

| Year | Corporate Income Tax Top Marginal Rates | Year | Corporate Income Tax Top Marginal Rates |
|---|---|---|---|
| 1953 | 52.0% | 1983 | 46.0% |
| 1954 | 52.0% | 1984 | 46.0% |
| 1955 | 52.0% | 1985 | 46.0% |
| 1956 | 52.0% | 1986 | 46.0% |
| 1957 | 52.0% | 1987 | 40.0% |
| 1958 | 52.0% | 1988 | 34.0% |
| 1959 | 52.0% | 1989 | 34.0% |
| 1960 | 52.0% | 1990 | 34.0% |
| 1961 | 52.0% | 1991 | 34.0% |
| 1962 | 52.0% | 1992 | 34.0% |
| 1963 | 52.0% | 1993 | 35.0% |
| 1964 | 50.0% | 1994 | 35.0% |
| 1965 | 48.0% | 1995 | 35.0% |
| 1966 | 48.0% | 1996 | 35.0% |
| 1967 | 48.0% | 1997 | 35.0% |
| 1968 | 52.8% | 1998 | 35.0% |
| 1969 | 52.8% | 1999 | 35.0% |
| 1970 | 49.2% | 2000 | 35.0% |
| 1971 | 48.0% | 2001 | 35.0% |
| 1972 | 48.0% | 2002 | 35.0% |
| 1973 | 48.0% | 2003 | 35.0% |
| 1974 | 48.0% | 2004 | 35.0% |
| 1975 | 48.0% | 2005 | 35.0% |
| 1976 | 48.0% | 2006 | 35.0% |
| 1977 | 48.0% | 2007 | 35.0% |
| 1978 | 48.0% | 2008 | 35.0% |
| 1979 | 46.0% | 2009 | 35.0% |
| 1980 | 46.0% | 2010 | 35.0% |
| 1981 | 46.0% | 2011 | 35.0% |
| 1982 | 46.0% | | |

**Source: Tax Policy Center**

## Civilian Labor Force Employment and Change in Employment
### 1953 - 2011

| Year | Civilian Labor Force | | Year | Civilian Labor Force | | |
|---|---|---|---|---|---|---|
| | Employed Total (1) (thousands) | Net Change in Employed (2) | | Employed Total (1) (thousands) | | Net Change in Employed (2) |
| 1953 | 61,600 | (1,576) | 1983 | 99,161 | | 4,040 |
| 1954 | 60,024 | 729 | 1984 | 103,201 | | 3,101 |
| 1955 | 60,753 | 3,000 | 1985 | 106,302 | | 2,585 |
| 1956 | 63,753 | (121) | 1986 | 108,887 | | 2,066 |
| 1957 | 63,632 | (412) | 1987 | 110,953 | | 3,063 |
| 1958 | 63,220 | 648 | 1988 | 114,016 | | 2,692 |
| 1959 | 63,868 | 1,479 | 1989 | 116,708 | | 2,373 |
| 1960 | 65,347 | 429 | 1990 | 119,081 | | (1,141) |
| 1961 | 65,776 | 332 | 1991 | 117,940 | | 38 |
| 1962 | 66,108 | 964 | 1992 | 117,978 | | 1,097 |
| 1963 | 67,072 | 1,255 | 1993 | 119,075 | | 2,891 |
| 1964 | 68,327 | 1,670 | 1994 | 121,966 | | 2,697 |
| 1965 | 69,997 | 2,201 | 1995 | 124,663 | | 462 |
| 1966 | 72,198 | 1,473 | 1996 | 125,125 | | 3,173 |
| 1967 | 73,671 | 1,029 | 1997 | 128,298 | | 2,428 |
| 1968 | 74,700 | 2,105 | 1998 | 130,726 | | 2,301 |
| 1969 | 76,805 | 1,975 | 1999 | 133,027 | | 3,532 |
| 1970 | 78,780 | 84 | 2000 | 136,559 | * | 1,219 |
| 1971 | 78,864 | 2,095 | 2001 | 137,778 | | (2,077) |
| 1972 | 80,959 | 2,202 | 2002 | 135,701 | | 1,716 |
| 1973 | 83,161 | 3,394 | 2003 | 137,417 | * | 1,055 |
| 1974 | 86,555 | (928) | 2004 | 138,472 | * | 1,773 |
| 1975 | 85,627 | 1,773 | 2005 | 140,245 | * | 2,905 |
| 1976 | 87,400 | 2,528 | 2006 | 143,150 | * | 2,878 |
| 1977 | 89,928 | 4,456 | 2007 | 146,028 | * | 369 |
| 1978 | 94,384 | 3,564 | 2008 | 146,397 | * | (4,210) |
| 1979 | 97,948 | 1,931 | 2009 | 142,187 | * | (3,687) |
| 1980 | 99,879 | 76 | 2010 | 138,500 | * | 830 |
| 1981 | 99,955 | (263) | 2011 | 139,330 | * | 2,307 |
| 1982 | 99,692 | (531) | 2012 | 141,637 | * | |

See Appendix C 1.2 for source of data

Notes to Appendix C 1.1
Civilian Labor Force Employment and Change in Employment
1953 - 2011


\* Data affected by change in population controls

(1) SOURCE - Bureau of Labor Statistics (BLS)
   Labor Force Statistics from the Current Population Survey,
      16 Years and Over, Seasonally Adjusted, January Report of Each Year
         Series Id: LNS12000000   Labor force status:  Employed
            (Data extracted on: March 17, 2012)


(2) Total employed in each year - total employed the preceding year

## Annual Labor Force Statistics by Presidential Term
### Jan, 1953 - Jan, 1989

| Year | Employed Total (1) (thousands) | Net Change in Employed | Year | Employed Total (1) (thousands) | Net Change in Employed |
|---|---|---|---|---|---|
| Eisenhower: Jan, 1953 - Jan, 1961 | | | Nixon / Ford: Jan, 1969 - Jan, 1977 | | |
| 1953 | 61,600 | (1,576) | 1969 | 76,805 | 1,975 |
| 1954 | 60,024 | 729 | 1970 | 78,780 | 84 |
| 1955 | 60,753 | 3,000 | 1971 | 78,864 | 2,095 |
| 1956 | 63,753 | (121) | 1972 | 80,959 | 2,202 |
| 1957 | 63,632 | (412) | 1973 | 83,161 | 3,394 |
| 1958 | 63,220 | 648 | 1974 | 86,555 | (928) |
| 1959 | 63,868 | 1,479 | 1975 | 85,627 | 1,773 |
| 1960 | 65,347 | 429 | 1976 | 87,400 | 2,528 |
| 1961 | 65,776 | 0 | 1977 | 89,928 | |
| Change | 4,176 | 4,176 | Change | 13,123 | 13,123 |
| Kennedy /Johnson: Jan, 1961- Jan, 1965 | | | Carter: Jan, 1977 - Jan. 1981 | | |
| 1961 | 65,776 | 332 | 1977 | 89,928 | 4,456 |
| 1962 | 66,108 | 964 | 1978 | 94,384 | 3,564 |
| 1963 | 67,072 | 1,255 | 1979 | 97,948 | 1,931 |
| 1964 | 68,327 | 1,670 | 1980 | 99,879 | 76 |
| 1965 | 69,997 | | 1981 | 99,955 | |
| Change | 4,221 | 4,221 | Change | 10,027 | 10,027 |
| Johnson: Jan, 1965- Jan, 1969 | | | Reagan: Jan, 1981 - Jan, 1989 | | |
| 1965 | 69,997 | 2,201 | 1981 | 99,955 | (263) |
| 1966 | 72,198 | 1,473 | 1982 | 99,692 | (531) |
| 1967 | 73,671 | 1,029 | 1983 | 99,161 | 4,040 |
| 1968 | 74,700 | 2,105 | 1984 | 103,201 | 3,101 |
| 1969 | 76,805 | | 1985 | 106,302 | 2,585 |
| Change | 6,808 | 6,808 | 1986 | 108,887 | 2,066 |
| | | | 1987 | 110,953 | 3,063 |
| | | | 1988 | 114,016 | 2,692 |
| | | | 1989 | 116,708 | |
| | | | Change | 16,753 | 16,753 |

(1) See Appendix C 1.1

## Annual Labor Force Statistics by Presidential Term
### Jan, 1989 - Jan, 2012

| Year | Employed Total (1) (thousands) | Net Change in Employed |
|---|---|---|
| Bush (1): Jan, 1989 - Jan, 1993 | | |
| 1989 | 116,708 | 2,373 |
| 1990 | 119,081 | (1,141) |
| 1991 | 117,940 | 38 |
| 1992 | 117,978 | 1,097 |
| 1993 | 119,075 | |
| Change | 2,367 | 2,367 |
| Clinton: Jan, 1993 - Jan, 2001 | | |
| 1993 | 119,075 | 2,891 |
| 1994 | 121,966 | 2,697 |
| 1995 | 124,663 | 462 |
| 1996 | 125,125 | 3,173 |
| 1997 | 128,298 | 2,428 |
| 1998 | 130,726 | 2,301 |
| 1999 | 133,027 | 3,532 |
| 2000 | 136,559 | 1,219 |
| 2001 | 137,778 | |
| Change | 18,703 | 18,703 |
| Bush (2): Jan, 2001 - Jan, 2009 | | |
| 2001 | 137,778 | (2,077) |
| 2002 | 135,701 | 1,716 |
| 2003 | 137,417 | 1,055 |
| 2004 | 138,472 | 1,773 |
| 2005 | 140,245 | 2,905 |
| 2006 | 143,150 | 2,878 |
| 2007 | 146,028 | 369 |
| 2008 | 146,397 | (4,210) |
| 2009 | 142,187 | |
| Change | 4,409 | 4,409 |

| Year | Employed Total (1) (thousands) | Net Change in Employed |
|---|---|---|
| Obama: Jan, 2009 - | | |
| 2009 | 142,187 | (3,687) |
| 2010 | 138,500 | 830 |
| 2011 | 139,330 | 2,307 |
| 2012 | 141,637 | |
| Change | (550) | (550) |

(1) See Appendix C 1.1

www.ingramcontent.com/pod-product-compliance
Lightning Source LLC
Chambersburg PA
CBHW081655270326
41933CB00017B/3182